T0347306

A Practical Guide to STAFF DEVELOPMENT & APPRAISAL in Schools

Kogan Page Books for Teachers Series

Career Development for Teachers, Jim Donnelly
Child Protection for Teachers and Schools, Ben Whitney
The Children Act and Schools, Ben Whitney
Education for Citizenship, edited by Eileen Baglin Jones and Neville Jones
A Guide to Creative Tutoring, Stephen Adams
A Handbook for Deputy Heads in Schools, Jim Donnelly
Learning to Behave, edited by Neville Jones and Eileen Baglin Jones
Making Science Education Relevant, Douglas P Newton
Mentoring in Schools, edited by Margaret Wilkin
Middle Managers in Schools and Colleges, Jim Donnelly
Modern Languages for All, Maggie Bovair and Keith Bovair
Parental Choice in Education, edited by Mark Halstead
A Practical Guide to Staff Development and Appraisal in Schools, Helen Horne and
    Anthony Pierce
Themes and Dimensions of the National Curriculum, edited by Geoffrey Hall
The Truth About Truancy, Ben Whitney

A
Practical Guide to
STAFF
DEVELOPMENT
& APPRAISAL
in Schools

HELEN HORNE
and
ANTHONY PIERCE

Routledge
Taylor & Francis Group

LONDON AND NEW YORK

First published 1996 by Kogan Page Limited

2 Park Square, Milton Park, Abingdon, Oxon OX14 4RN
711 Third Avenue, New York, NY 10017, USA

Routledge is an imprint of the Taylor & Francis Group, an informa business

First issued in hardback 2016

British Library Cataloguing in Publication Data

A CIP record for this book is available from the British Library

ISBN 978-1-138-15997-6 (hbk)
ISBN 978-0-7494-1780-2 (pbk)

Typeset by Jo Brereton, Primary Focus, Bradford

Contents

Acknowledgements

We would like to acknowledge the help of the following people in the writing of this book.

All the staff of Haydon Bridge High School, Northumberland, with particular reference to David Thompson, Barbara Mansfield, Ruth Hudspith, Lynne West and Keith Rowesby; David Watson, Allendale Middle School, Northumberland; John Lambert, Allendale First School, Northumberland; Gordon Wellans, Inglewood Junior School, Cumbria; all the staff at William Howard School, Cumbria, with particular reference to Roger Alston, Janet Simpson and Pam Butler; staff at Trinity School, Cumbria, including Terry Dyer; all the staff at Kenton School, Newcastle, with particular reference to Jenny Robinson; staff at the Newman School, Cumbria, with particular reference to Gerald Richardson; Jo Brereton of Primary Focus for the DTP work; Sally Brown of the University of Northumbria; Clive Pepper, Phil Whitehead, Chris Marsh and other colleagues in Buckinghamshire schools; Joanne Smith of Cherry Tree School, Bolton and all the hundreds of teachers and headteachers who have freely given their advice, information and time; Duncan Graham and Alan Evans for inspiration! And finally, Jo and Roger on dinner duty – without their sustenance none of this would have happened!

Helen Horne and
Anthony Pierce
Spring 1996

Introduction

AN HISTORICAL PERSPECTIVE – WHERE DID TEACHER APPRAISAL COME FROM?

The history of the development of teacher appraisal can be traced back to the early 1970s or even earlier. This history is well documented elsewhere but, as the remit of this book is to look forward rather than backward, we shall not dwell on historical perspectives. However, for those joining appraisal for the first time, or those who may have forgotten what it is really about, we will familiarise you with the origins of the process.

During the industrial disputes which ravaged the teaching profession in the 1980s the issue of teacher appraisal was never far from the surface. Stoked by the former Secretary of State for Education, Sir Keith Joseph, the fires of performance appraisal were always near the forefront. This was predicted by many to be introduced as a way of sorting the good, the bad and the incompetent. In 1986 representatives of the LEAs, the professional associations and the DES (DfEE) met under the auspices of ACAS to determine a process by which appraisal could be introduced into schools for the benefit of all. A National Steering Group was established to trial appraisal in six LEAs between 1986 and 1989. These disparate LEAs – Cumbria, Salford, Newcastle upon Tyne, Somerset, Suffolk and Croydon – did an immense amount of work guided by their Chairman Duncan Graham who, when CEO in Suffolk, had been responsible for encouraging the possibilities of a positive approach to appraisal in schools.

The outcome of the pilot was to produce a National Framework for appraisal which broadly had the support of all those groups involved in its production. This 1989 National Framework proposed the introduction of a national appraisal system which was developmental. Kenneth Baker, Secretary of State for Education, was on the point of introducing appraisal in a Statutory Framework when he was moved to the Home Office and replaced by John MacGregor, who decided not to introduce statutory appraisal as he felt schools were already coping with sufficient change from the various Education Acts of the time.

Finally, in July 1991, Kenneth Clarke as Secretary of State for Education took the Teacher Appraisal Regulations through Parliament. These Regulations spelt out the legal position, and were ably supported by Circular 12/91 from the DfEE. These two documents, taken together, still form the backbone of the appraisal process and have never been amended. A copy of both documents was made available to all schools and, together with any documentation issued by LEAs, are what appraisal is based on today. Throughout this book we refer extensively to Circular 12/91 and to the Regulations.

The language of appraisal is fairly simple, the only potential complication being the terminology of the appraisal interview as the DfEE describe it. The six appraisal pilots each had their own name for this part of the process. *Discussion, conference* and *meeting* were three terms used and perhaps *discussion* was the most meaningful. However, as the DfEE chose *interview* we have used this term, though we feel that *discussion* or *meeting* are more appropriate. Similarly, the terms *targets, objectives* and *goals* have been used for those development activities which emerge after the interview. We have chosen to stay with the term *targets.*

We offer the following model as a stereotype of what is now happening for most teachers in the appraisal process. It contains all the required elements of the Regulations and all the suggestions of Circular 12/91, plus good ideas from teachers actually being appraised and appraising. We hope it is useful. Steps one to five take place in year one. Step six takes place both in year one and in year two of the two-year cycle.

- Step one
  Awareness raising and introduction to appraisal, the aims, processes and links with school development plans.

- Step two
  Broad self-appraisal using the job description, and any useful documentation provided by the LEA or school.

- Step three
  Initial meeting between appraiser and appraisee to set ground rules for the process, agree dates, decide on a focus or focuses.

- Step four
  Classroom observation (or Task for headteachers), which is compulsory, and other data collection, which is optional.

- Step five
  The appraisal interview and target setting.

- Step six
  Meetings between appraiser and appraisee to review progress on the targets. The Regulations require one meeting before the end of the second year of the two-year cycle but we would recommend several regular meetings.

APPRAISAL IN THE SECOND CYCLE AND BEYOND – AN OVERVIEW

In July 1991 the Aims for the National Appraisal Scheme for teachers were published by the DfEE as part of the Education (School Teacher Appraisal) Regulations. The aims stated:

1. Appraisal bodies shall secure that appraisal assists:
   (a) school teachers in their professional development and career planning; and
   (b) those responsible for taking decisions about the management of school teachers.
2. In carrying out their duty... appraising bodies shall aim to improve the quality of education for pupils, through assisting school teachers to realise their potential and to carry out their duties more effectively.
3. Appraisal procedures shall in particular aim to:
   (a) recognise the achievements of school teachers and help them identify ways of improving their skills and performance;
   (b) help school teachers, governing bodies and LEAs (as the case may be) to determine whether a change of duties would help the professional development of school teachers and improve their career prospects;
   (c) identify the potential of teachers for career development with the aim of helping them, where possible, through appropriate in-service training;
   (d) help school teachers having difficulty with their performance through appropriate guidance counselling and training;
   (e) inform those responsible for providing references for school teachers in relation to appointments;
   (f) improve the management of schools.

So after five years have the aims been achieved? Has some of the scepticism which greeted appraisal been assuaged? Has it improved the quality of learning for pupils?

As expected there is a mixed answer to all the questions and in later chapters we explore the answers in more detail, but some facts have clearly emerged:

- The government has not sought to change the aims of appraisal.
- The government did keep to its agreements for funding the introduction of appraisal.
- The timetable through to July 1995 has been broadly kept to by LEAs and schools.
- Many teachers have benefited from the process, though some have not, both for a variety of reasons.
- There are increasing links between the individual benefits that can be achieved from appraisal and the benefits schools can gain.
- The process is here to stay.
- There are increasing links between appraisal and teaching and learning. We strongly believe that strengthening these links will guarantee a future for appraisal. The Teacher Training Agency and the government see appraisal as a way of improving schools and in particular improving the quality of teaching and learning. If appraisal is used as a mechanism through which teachers can focus on their activities related to this core function, then it will have a future. If not, the future is bleak.
- Maintaining the momentum of appraisal after the first cycle is difficult in some schools.
- Many teachers are now beginning the second or even third cycle of appraisal – some cheerfully, some reluctantly.

Our goal in this book is to provide as much help as possible to appraisees, appraisers and those who manage the process, as they move on to second and third appraisal cycles at a time when there is no direct funding to do so. This book is written to reflect on what has happened since 1991. We also offer best practice based on our research and practice in schools. We begin by considering some of the main issues for those involved in appraisal in 1996 and beyond.

FUNDING

Between 1991 and 1995 the government provided about £54 million for the introduction of appraisal and they have since made it clear that there will be no more direct funding. The money, provided through GEST, was for pump priming. Government now expects appraisal to form part of the day-to-day working life of teachers as it does for many other people. In the financial year 1995–6 appraisal was a valid expenditure heading under Activity 1, School Effectiveness. In 1996–7 there is no such guarantee. So appraisal has had to fight for resources with other equally justifiable claimants. Perhaps the real argument about funding appraisal is not how much will the government provide, but how much of the funding that we have available in schools can we, or will we, spend on appraisal as a way of lubricating and supplying other needs.

The main problem with funding is that of classroom observation. How are schools with all their staff engaged in full-time teaching supposed to find someone to teach the appraiser's class while she/he is observing an appraisee? Some secondary schools may solve the problem at present by colleagues covering for each other but this goodwill will not last forever. In the primary sector, often with no non-contact time allocated, this is impossible. Special schools, too, have their individual problems. We do not believe there is a satisfactory answer to classroom observation without dedicated funding, whether this comes from government or school.

Schools are, however, maintaining observation despite this problem, often through the headteacher or heads of department undertaking the cover. This does not of course work where the headteacher or departmental head has a full-time teaching commitment. One way around this is that the school funds the observation from other sources in its control. In order to do this the schools have to decide what value they place on appraisal in working towards their vision, as appraisal is only one available mechanism through which schools can achieve their goals.

If a school places a high priority on the possible benefits of appraisal helping to *achieve the aims* declared earlier in the chapter, then the costs of appraisal will have a *high priority in the school development plan*. Appraisal remains a statutory responsibility and a part of the OFSTED Framework. In our experience the level of priority given to appraisal has a direct correlation with how its success has been viewed in the past, and whether effective monitoring and evaluation have taken place.

What does appraisal cost? Strong advocates of appraisal argue that *cost* is only one side of the equation and it must be balanced against the *benefits*. To do this requires an evaluation of whether appraisal has achieved its aims. How many schools have carried out such evaluations?

If you assume that all appraisal meetings take place in the 1265 statutory working hours, but outside contact time, then the only money cost is supply cover for the observation. This works out at approximately £30 per hour, or per appraisal, over a two-year cycle. Is this too much to pay? Idealism we hear you cry. It's impossible to look at it like that. You can't get a supply teacher in just for an hour, but there are ways to manage this which we address throughout the book.

We are not necessarily supporting the idea of all appraisal taking place in so-called non-contact 1265 time, but we know it does happen, and very successfully, in cases where appraisal is not viewed as a bolt-on activity but as a part of improving life for all in school. The real answer with cost is that appraisal has to show real benefit, just like every other aspect of school life. To do this *benefits must be identified*. If appraisal meets its aims, then benefits will accrue in the school, leading ultimately to improved teacher morale, improved teaching standards and an environment in which learning for all is meaningful and not rhetoric.

A further aspect of cost is the funding of the outcomes of appraisal. It could well be argued that appraisal outcomes should lead to clearer identification of development and training needs. If this is the case it should also lead to more targeted expenditure. More research than is at present available needs to be conducted into this.

The funding debate will doubtlessly continue but we would suggest, as schools plan their budgets, that the cost of the appraisal process ought to be given credence alongside other headings. We also suggest that whoever is responsible for appraisal in schools does spend time on a cost–benefit analysis for appraisal which is communicated to all staff. We know of schools which have been surprised by the outcome of this and others for whom the analysis has confirmed their original thoughts.

TIME

Teachers will always say there isn't enough time for appraisal and this has to be acknowledged. In looking at the time needed for appraisal, some basic questions need to be asked by appraisees and appraisers.

- What do I want out of appraisal for myself (eg a meaningful process)?
- What do I want out of appraisal for the school (or department or team)?
- What benefits do I want from appraisal (eg inspired teaching and learning)?
- How can these be identified?

Having answered these the next question is:

- In order to get what I want, how much time am I prepared to invest?

From a school management perspective the question that has to be answered is:

- How much time are we prepared to invest in the staff in order for them to achieve what they want or, perhaps more importantly, need, to do their job with the utmost effectiveness?

Having worked out the answers to this, people can set about looking at what they can really do with appraisal. We have determined that on average the time taken for an appraisal in the first year of the cycle is roughly as shown in the box.

	Appraisee	**Appraiser**
Initial meeting	30 minutes	30 minutes
Observation to include immediate feedback	90 minutes	90 minutes
Interview	60 minutes	60 minutes
Total	**180 minutes**	**180 minutes**

The above times do not include self-appraisal, but can you really quantify such time? However, they do include writing the statement and targets during the interview. A model for this is included on page 42.

To some readers three hours may seem a very long time for appraisal in the first year of its cycle, to others not long enough. This is why a cost–benefit analysis must be undertaken to show the value or otherwise. For the appraisee the three hours is probably not as great an issue as for the appraiser. An appraiser with say four appraisals to carry out has twelve hours or more work. Can this be justified? What has to go from their job description or profile to enable this to happen? It may be that the job profile has to be rewritten to include appraiser time if the role of appraiser is considered of sufficient importance. Is another alternative to increase the numbers of appraisers and therefore spread the load more widely? Or to have a school culture in which people see their work as an appraiser as a really useful part of their own professional development and want to put in the time for this work?

What is clear is that of the three hours indicated only one of the hours has to be done in direct contact time, ie the observation. We mentioned earlier that you cannot bring in a supply teacher for one-hour sessions. But you can arrange a number of observations on one day, thus making effective use of supply time. It can be argued that it does not suit everyone to have observation on the same day but this is a better solution than colleagues trying to cover and classes being doubled up.

Another solution to the time problem is to offset or disaggregate INSET time against appraisal time. In other words, the requirement to be present for five days INSET time is reduced by the amount of time needed to be put into appraisal over a year, say half a day. This time can be used for the process or simply counted against it. This is using 1265 creatively.

Many teachers have found with appraisal that the question is not how much time something takes, but how effectively and efficiently that time is used. If each part of the process is planned, with an agenda, start time and finish time, then time can be saved and people's attitudes improved.

Many teachers have put in far more time for appraisal than we have suggested – if this has been worthwhile, fair enough. If not, there needs to be an evaluation of why not, and action taken to improve things, perhaps along the lines suggested.

MATCHING APPRAISERS WITH APPRAISEES

This issue is crucial. Unless appraiser and appraisee are well matched and can trust each other they should not work together. Matching should be sensitive, understood and agreed by all involved.

A question we are often asked is whether appraiser and appraisee should continue working together into the second cycle. There is no definitive answer. Practice, however, tells us that where the two wish to continue together and where there are perceived benefits for this to happen, there is no reason why it should not. We suggest that at the start of the first cycle of working together both appraiser and appraisee agree that this will initially be for one cycle and will then be mutually reviewed, with the headteacher, without any prejudice.

An issue that has rumbled around is that of the quality of the appraisers and how well they do their job of appraising. Without doubt the best person to judge whether the appraiser is doing the job well is the appraisee. It may be an idea for schools to define a criteria for all appraisers to work towards and receive feedback on this from the appraisee. We believe that every appraiser should ask their appraisees to offer them constructive feedback on their work as an appraiser, specifying particular points they want feedback on. We also believe every appraisee should offer to give such feedback. The feedback is then not one sided, with the appraiser giving feedback while the appraisee is the receiver. Surely the art of giving and receiving constructive feedback has to be good for both parties.

THIRD-PARTY DATA COLLECTION

The use of third-party data collection is an option in teacher appraisal but unlike classroom observation it is not compulsory. Data collection has been used in some teacher appraisals but probably more in headteacher appraisal, and those teachers with a management focus have tended to use it more than those with a teaching focus. There is a move in industrial appraisal from a performance-related model to a developmental model, as used by teachers. In many processes, observation is not compulsory and information is collected from those closest to the employees at work. This includes managers, customers, and those for whom the appraisee is responsible. By asking such people to contribute to the appraisal, a 360° view can be obtained. Could a move to observation and/or data collection in teacher appraisal be timely? Reactions over the last few years to data collection have predictably been mixed. To some it has been far more use than observation but others have doubted its honesty. Both appraisees and appraisers have found the time spent on data collection immense – but highly rewarding. If data collection is used, we suggest it should have a number of criteria:

- No data should be collected unless the Code of Practice from Circular 12/91 is followed.
- There must be a real purpose to collecting data in this way.
- All data collected should be open to the appraisee.
- There should be a time limit for this part of the process.

As teachers move into the second and subsequent cycles of appraisal, we suggest that data collection from people giving a 360° perspective may find a greater place in the process. Many schools which are involved in the Investors in People Standard (IIP) have already started a programme of appraisal to form the annual review for all staff required by IIP. For non-teachers classroom observation is inappropriate and great use can be made of data collection.

TARGETS

Every teacher has the right to know if their targets will be met in full or in part and on what time scale. Teachers should not be left for weeks without hearing anything and the management of appraisal in a school should ensure this does not happen. The whole issue of target setting needs careful attention. For too many teachers targets have become little more than an add-on at the end of the interview, or something that would be useful, but which will never be achieved in reality. The way to tackle this is for every teacher to be aware of the available resources which can be used to meet targets.

Teachers who have been involved in producing the school development plan will have a sense of ownership of this and a heightened awareness of what might be achieved in targets, but others are working in the dark.

MONITORING AND EVALUATION

Paragraph 71 of Circular 12/91 makes clear the arrangements that should be made for monitoring and periodic evaluation of appraisals. A simple checklist is sufficient for monitoring and should include the following:

Name of appraisee:

Name of appraiser:

Appraisal activity:

Date:

Under the activity, a list is made of the compulsory parts of appraisal and the optional ones to be used, eg data collection. As each part is completed, the date is entered in the appropriate column and the process monitored.

JOB DESCRIPTIONS

Circular 12/91 states in Paragraph 19 that appraisal should be undertaken on the basis of an established job description. Most teachers have such a document and increasingly it is an active rather than a passive document, in many cases becoming known as a profile. For those teachers without a job description or profile the annual teachers pay and conditions of service document has always been the accepted basis for appraisal and will probably continue to be so. Some teachers have been given the opportunity of redefining their job through the appraisal process.

THE LENGTH OF THE APPRAISAL CYCLE

An appraisal cycle is two years, with the main activity taking place in year one and a meeting at least once before the end of the second year to review progress made towards achieving targets. In the second year of the cycle it is advantageous to have several meetings, otherwise progress towards targets will be somewhat limited. Outside teaching most appraisal cycles are annual and there seems to be a trend – in practice, if not on paper – to make the teachers' cycle annual. Where appraisal is being really effective we feel certain that it has become what ACAS, in setting up the process, intended it to be:

> The working group (ACAS) understands appraisal not as a series of perfunctory events, but as a continuous and systematic process intended to help individual teachers with their professional development and career planning, and to ensure that the in-service training and deployment of teachers matches the complementary needs of individual teachers and schools.
>
> ACAS 1986

WHY APPRAISAL?

The aims of appraisal are clear. All teachers can benefit from them if they wish and if the school organises appraisal as a meaningful process. Success depends on commitment from the head of the school, an effective coordinator and the support of individual staff. Without this appraisal will be a process which has to be undertaken purely because it is a statutory requirement.

1

The Appraisal Cycle

People work more effectively when they know what is expected of them... if they know that their performance is being monitored by a boss who is prepared to be honest with them at least once a year, but hopefully more frequently.

Ron Shepherd, training manager of the Ford Motor Company, quoted in the City of Newcastle upon Tyne's appraisal pilot document

This raises two very important areas of questioning surrounding the whole notion of appraisal. The first area is related to expectations. Who expects what and from whom? People are increasingly expected to do the right thing, first time, every time, in their job. Appraisal may, therefore, be viewed as a means of assessing how far such expectations are being met. This in turn raises the question of teacher competencies, and performance related pay rears its uncomfortable head. While the unions appear to have reassured their members, most LEAs insert the proviso in their appraisal documentation that, 'there will be no automatic link between appraisal and promotion or additions to salary' but add that they feel it is both 'legitimate and desirable for headteachers to take into account information from appraisal, in advising governors on decisions on promotions and pay'. This statement is specifically made as Appraisal Regulation 14 of Circular 12/91.

The second question is that concerning the appraisal cycle. How frequently should a teacher be appraised? While the sentiments expressed above by Ron Shepherd may still send shivers of apprehension down some teachers' spines, they would also not be acceptable to many headteachers, in terms of their diminishing school budgets, rising curriculum expenditure and the pressing demands of LMS. However, as we stated in the Introduction, for some teachers the cycle is becoming annual. One reason is that the conditions under which schools operate are changing so rapidly, even an annual cycle may be too long. The review meeting, required in the second year of the cycle, is now often being used almost as a second professional discussion.

The original proposal for a two-year cycle came from the National Framework for Teacher Appraisal which states in paragraph 27 that:

> In considering the question of how frequently appraisal should take place we have aimed to identify a framework that is manageable for individual teachers and headteachers, taking into account the current pressures on schools; but which also ensures a genuinely continuous and systematic process, of maximum benefit to teachers and schools, bearing these aims in mind we recommend that the appraisal of both headteachers and teachers be conducted in a two-year cycle.

While schools have followed the letter of the National Framework, embodied in Regulations, and introduced a system of appraisal broadly in line with its recommendations in terms of the components of the appraisal system, they have not yet followed the spirit of the recommendations in terms of linking appraisal, not only to the needs of the individual, but also to the needs of the school. If the stated aims of any appraisal system are to improve the quality of education for pupils, in terms of the quality of teaching and learning, we now need to move forward into firmly linking appraisal systems to school development planning, not only to 'match' but also to identify these 'complementary needs of the individual teachers and the schools'.

Some LEA appraisal documents have clearly outlined links with appraisal and school development plans, stating that appraisal should be set in the context of the school's objectives, generally expressed in the school development plan, and should support development planning and vice versa. This is sometimes elaborated by suggesting that targets should meet school needs as well as individual and that when targets are taken together they should provide an important agenda for action for the whole school. This will improve the quality of teaching and learning in the context of a whole school environment, which will lead to an all-pervading atmosphere and ethos of 'school improvement'. These statements help to adjust the emphasis of the concept of appraisal from its present individual focus into a more collective dimension. This theme was recommended in the 1995 Evaluation of Appraisal conducted on behalf of the DfEE and is currently being explored by the Teacher Training Agency. It is also a theme which pervades this book.

COMPONENTS OF THE APPRAISAL CYCLE

All schools have followed the National Framework recommendations for the appraisal process which drew on the experience of the six pilot projects and were embodied in the Appraisal Regulations and Circular 12/91. There are seven elements to be included in the process, either compulsory or recommended. Those in **bold** type below are compulsory for teachers. For headteachers the initial meeting is added to the list.

- **an initial meeting between appraiser and appraisee (NB compulsory for headteachers only** – recommended for teachers);
- self-appraisal;
- **classroom observation;**
- collection of data from other sources, agreed by the appraisee;
- **an appraisal interview, in which professional targets for action are agreed;**
- **the preparation of an appraisal statement,** to be agreed by both parties;
- follow-up, including **a formal review meeting in the second year of the cycle.**

The extent to which these guidelines are rigidly adhered to varies from authority to authority and school to school. Some schools have amalgamated several of the components and have devised a four-point plan of:

- preparation;
- collection of data;
- the interview;
- follow-up and monitoring.

In this model the preparation component involves the appraiser in contracting and negotiating for the forthcoming collection of information, classroom observation, interview and any subsequent action. The collection of data section recommends that the data, relevant to the appraisal process, will be collected by the appraiser, appraisee and others whose contribution has been agreed. This model also suggests that classroom observation and any self-appraisal form part of this section of the process. It also recommends that the appraisal interview should be concerned with the appraiser and appraisee meeting to review the data collected and then to identify areas for the appraisee's professional development and to set targets enabling those needs to be met. The final stage refers to the follow-up and monitoring sections as a formal review meeting. It is suggested that this follow-up must be carried out in order to assess the progress towards the developmental targets agreed in the interview. This part of the process needs as much credence as the other stages if appraisal is to be meaningful to all concerned and to stand a chance of contributing towards improvements in teaching and learning.

As all schools are using these components of the appraisal cycle we will explore each in turn. We take as our starting point not the initial meeting but self-appraisal. This is because a constructive meeting will more easily be achieved if the appraisee has benefited from some form of self-appraisal beforehand to inform the subsequent discussions and areas of focus. We will also combine the classroom observation sections with other data collection as these are linked, forming the basis of a constructive appraisal interview and target setting. Therefore, our model is a five-point plan:

- general self-appraisal for both participants;
- initial meeting – followed by specific self-appraisal;
- classroom observation and data collection;
- interview including target setting and statement writing;
- follow-up and formal review.

SELF-APPRAISAL

The ACAS report stated that 'each appraisal should be preceded and informed by self-appraisal'. The pilot LEAs also emphasised the importance of self-appraisal as a key part of the process. This view has been reinforced by many teachers as both a necessary and valuable component of appraisal. Circular 12/91, however, does not insist that self-appraisal is compulsory but does advise that teachers reflect on their own performance to inform the subsequent discussion. What has emerged, for many teachers, is the value of a general self-appraisal based on their job description and all other aspects of their work. The initial self-appraisal carried out prior to the initial meeting may lead to a teacher identifying one or more areas of focus. After the initial meeting, when the appraisal focus has been agreed, more structured self-appraisal can take place, concentrating on the agreed specific focus (as shown in Figure 1.1).

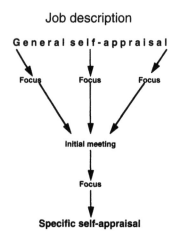

Figure 1.1 *The stages of self-appraisal*

We explore both phases of self-appraisal in detail.

General self-appraisal

The purpose of self-appraisal is to prepare for, and contribute to, the overall process and it is recommended to both appraisers and appraisees alike. There are good reasons for this as it:

- helps the appraisee to think about the main elements of their job;
- helps the appraisee not only to dwell on areas of success and strength but also to explore areas for future development;
- gives the appraisee a voice in the appraisal process and develops a sense of ownership;
- helps to avoid suggestions that the process is a passive activity, 'done to' appraisees;
- helps to begin to identify possible areas of focus;
- helps to consider and examine the appraisee's job description;
- provides information and evidence to assist in the process;
- helps set the agenda for the initial meeting;
- helps to consider how other parts of the appraisal process will be managed.

Self-appraisal should be related to arriving at the focus or focuses of the appraisal. An area of focus needs to have been thought about at this early stage if appraisal is to fulfil the needs of the teacher as well as addressing the aims outlined in the school's development plan.

Since the overall purpose of self-appraisal is to help preparation for the rest of the process there is no need to have a written record for the appraiser. It is up to the appraisee to determine the extent and form of any feedback given from general self-appraisal. Self-appraisal provides an opportunity for the individual to set parts of the agenda, so that the process is driven primarily by the appraisee's needs, hopefully within a school context. The appraisal system needs the perspective of the individual teacher in order to fuel the dual initiatives of individual staff development and whole school planning. The information gathered from the appraisal process ought to enable the school's development plans to be driven by both the needs of the individual teacher and the prioritised needs of the school as identified by OFSTED, the National Curriculum and the stated aims of the school.

By engaging in general self-appraisal an individual has an opportunity to review, pause and reflect on vital and valuable personal experience. Many teachers may feel these experiences are no longer valued in their work. A good appraisal system will make sure they *are* valued. If this individual assessment opportunity is not taken it could be argued that the person is abdicating responsibility, though it is probably more attributable to exhaustion! By handing over control entirely to the appraiser the appraisee is denying him or herself a voice.

Although the initial self-appraisal takes place at the start of the process, in reality it ought to occur throughout the cycle, particularly during the few weeks that cover the intensive part of the process. For most teachers, informal self-appraisal happens naturally even if sometimes subconsciously. We constantly ask ourselves such questions as: How am I doing? How did that lesson go? What is going well in my work? Where can things be improved? What support do I need? Where will the time come from? It could be argued that self-appraisal is already continuous.

General self-appraisal capitalises on these natural questions. If it is slightly formalised, through the use of a documentation framework, it can give impetus to the process making it an active exercise rather than a passive experience.

There are many possible methods to use in general self-appraisal which can be helpful. These range from free writing about the job to the use of prompt sheets. In most schools it is up to appraisees to choose the format they find most appropriate. Some self-appraisal prompt sheets are a list of possible questions to ask oneself about work over the past year; others simply contain three or four questions. You may find the following examples useful, as amalgamations of best practice from a variety of schools and LEAs.

Self-appraisal Prompt List Towards a Classroom Focus

Reflect on the sections below in terms of your effectiveness in each area.

Working in the classroom

Is your preparation appropriate in terms of:
- class needs;
- group needs;
- individual needs;
- consideration of curriculum development;
- follow-up between lessons.

Classroom organisation

Is the layout and management of the class/classroom effective in:
- utilising a variety of teaching strategies;
- making instructions and expectations clear;
- providing well-organised and accessible resources;
- matching work to pupils' needs and abilities;
- the degree of responsibility the pupils take for their learning;
- record keeping.

General points

Taking a general overview of your classroom practice, what do you think of:
- the general atmosphere in lessons;
- the environment for your pupils;
- the quality of relationships – teacher–pupil, pupil–pupil;
- the balance of attention given to pupils with varying needs;
- control of the classroom situation;
- knowledge of the curriculum being delivered;
- interest aroused in the pupils.

Figure 1.2 *Effective self-appraisal in the classroom*

Self-appraisal – Questionnaire Model

Introduction
This model is designed in the form of a questionnaire. Asking a direct question may encourage greater clarity in the appraisee's initial response. Often an initial response is the best one to follow at this stage rather than spending a long time pondering!

1. What general comment would I make about my work over the past year?

2. What aspect of my work did I feel pleased about and what has given me job satisfaction?

3. What has not developed as well as I would have liked?

4. What has helped my work?

5. What has hindered my work?

6. How can I make my teaching more effective?

7. What areas of my work do I want to develop in the coming year?

8. What support do I need to carry out my duties effectively?

9. What are my professional development needs?

10. In what ways would I like my career to develop?

Figure 1.3 *Self-appraisal – questionnaire model*

Self-appraisal/Interview Preparation Form

1. What do you think are the main tasks and responsibilities of your current post?

2. During the past year, what parts of your job have given you greatest satisfaction?

   How are these being used to their best advantage?
   How could these be used to best advantage?

3. What parts of your job have given you least satisfaction?

   Why?

4. What problems or difficulties prevented you from achieving something you intended or hoped to do?

5. To help improve your performance in your job, what changes in the school organisation would be beneficial?

6. What do you think should be your main target(s)/goals for next year?

7. How would you like to see your career developing?

Figure 1.4 *Self-appraisal/interview preparation form*

Characteristics of Effective Teaching

(This is for guidance only; it is not a checklist and should not be used as such)

Appraisees are asked to look at each of the statements and respond to them in the most honest way. This will produce a profile of achievements and weaknesses which can then be explored as a possible appraisal focus.

Planning and preparation

Should...

- ensure that all students have access to the National Curriculum for a reasonable time;
- reflect a curriculum which is broad, balanced, relevant, differentiated and which has regard to equal opportunities;
- consider evidence and assess the needs of individual groups;
- indicate that activities are matched to ability and age;
- have clear aims including:
    - introduction
    - planned development of activities
    - extension/support ideas;
- consider the use of varied and appropriate equipment and resources;
- link activities with departmental / school schemes to ensure continuity in the learning process;
- link aspects across the whole curriculum;
- show awareness of the obligation to record and report the personal, educational and social achievements of pupils.

Learning and teaching strategies

Should...

- meet the needs of individual pupils regardless of race, creed, gender or ability;
- enable students to achieve success and make progress;
- communicate to pupils the aims of the lesson/activities;
- make appropriate and effective use of the teacher's expertise, resources and teaching aids;
- involve pupils in their own learning, by encouraging them to:
    - use their previous knowledge and experience
    - use their ideas and questions
    - predict the consequences of their actions
    - think for themselves
    - evaluate and improve both the processes and product of their work;

- recognise the importance of:
  - starting the lesson activity successfully by engaging the pupils' attention
  - maintaining purposeful involvement of the pupils
  - moving effectively from one activity to another
  - bringing the lesson to a satisfactory conclusion.

Classroom organisation and management

Should...

- manage the arrival of the students;
- ensure knowledge of and adherence to general classroom procedures by pupils and teacher;
- clearly indicate an active working environment;
- translate into practice what has been planned;
- make resources accessible to all pupils;
- make use of displays reflecting differing presentations and achievement levels, showing progression and celebrating success;
- give due attention to health and safety issues;
- manage the departure of pupils.

Assessment and evaluation

Should...

- make use of assessment data in the planning process;
- involve pupils in their own assessment and recording;
- inform pupils clearly of their level of achievement;
- suggest strategies for improvement;
- meet the needs of individual pupils;
- reflect stated objectives;
- match assessment to teaching and learning styles;
- keep appropriate records;
- inform parents at appropriate time.

Figure 1.5 *Characteristics of effective teaching*

General Self-appraisal

Classroom practice

- How well do I ensure that pupils know and understand the National Curriculum attainment targets and the appropriate programmes of study?

Applying the subject

- How do I know that I produce coherent lesson plans which take account of NCATs and the school's curriculum policies?
- How do I ensure continuity and progression in my teaching and learning opportunities for all pupils?

Managing pupils/relationships

- Do I establish clear expectations of behaviour and maintain these in practice at all times?
- How do I know that I create and maintain a purposeful, orderly and supportive environment?
- What do I do to devise and use appropriate rewards and sanctions to maintain an effective learning environment?

Teaching strategies

- Do I employ a range of teaching strategies appropriate to the age, ability and attainment level of pupils? What evidence do I have?
- How do I ensure that I take account of individual, group and whole class needs in my teaching and learning?
- How do I know that I will set appropriately demanding expectations for pupils?
- Do I communicate clearly and effectively with pupils through questioning, instructing, explaining and feedback? How do I know? What evidence do I have? How can I find out?

Assessment of pupils' progress

- What do I do to identify the current level of attainment of individual pupils? How often do I check this?

Future development

- Do I have an understanding of my role in the school? Who communicates this to me? How often is it reviewed?
- Am I clear as to my future role in the school? What do I want the role to be? Who can I discuss this with?

Figure 1.6 *General self-appraisal*

Effective Teaching and Learning

Appraisees are asked to consider how they feel about their work in relation to the points made below and to ask what evidence they have to support that view. Again, use initial reactions rather than a considered view.

Performance indicators

Variety and range of materials and approaches
- a broad range of materials is available to ensure access to the curriculum;
- a variety of resources is available to fit individual needs;
- different pupils are working on different tasks;
- materials and approaches are targeted appropriately at individual pupils;
- a range of appropriate learning activities is available and appropriately used, ie:
     structured reading and writing tasks
     investigational, open-ended work
     individualised programmes of work
     collaborative group work
     experiential learning.

Motivation and enthusiasm
- pupils are fully involved in the task;
- pupils are participating fully in the activity;
- pupils are engaged in a learning experience;
- pupils are discussing task or activity;
- pupils know what is expected of them and can explain the task;
- evidence of teacher giving praise, instructive criticism, enthusiastic encouragement and developing positive and supportive tone;
- pupil confidence and self-esteem are high.

Individual needs: differentiation
- teacher has knowledge of pupils' ability, learning patterns and personality;
- learning outcomes are matched to the individual pupils' needs, ability, interest and aptitude;
- teacher communicating with individuals and/or small groups;
- time allowed for pupils to complete a task varies according to individual difference;
- support and extension is systematically planned.

Classroom management: learning environment, classroom organisation
- the physical layout of the room should be appropriate for learning activity;
- there should be evidence of routines for the beginnings and endings of lessons;
- pupils should know what behaviour is expected of them for a variety of learning activities;
- pupils' work should be displayed in a way which shows it is valued;
- other displays should provide a stimulus for learning;
- a working atmosphere is maintained through effective communication between teacher and pupils;

- inappropriate behaviour is responded to appropriately and consistently; there is consistent use of sanctions and rewards;
- teacher responds to unexpected or unplanned situations.

Planning and preparation
- selection of educational aims and objectives in terms of learning outcomes for a lesson/number of lessons;
- approaches and resources are prepared and provided to deliver these;
- progression for individual pupils is built into the tasks/activities;
- evidence that the lesson/number of lessons is part of a structured course.

Communication: teacher presentation
- teacher makes clear the structure and purpose of the learning experience;
- the teacher is successful in engaging the pupils in the learning experience;
- the teacher uses a variety of ways of communicating, ie:
  informing
  describing
  explaining
  discussion
  questioning
- appropriate interventions in the pupil's learning experiences;
- pupils discuss work they are undertaking – this is part of the learning process.

Evaluation and reflection
- evidence of teacher evaluating recent experience and using information to determine future practice;
- evidence of evaluation of pupil work and progress being related to individual pupils;
- use of evidence collected by 'critical friend' promoting dialogue and reflection.

Pupil participation, involvement, responsibility
- pupils are involved in determining and identifying their own learning outcomes;
- where appropriate, pupils are given opportunities to choose the task, resources required and the way in which they work;
- pupils can identify and carry out appropriate behaviour in a variety of learning activities.

Assessment
- evidence of mechanisms for both formative and summative assessment;
- assessment is part of teaching and learning and is built into classroom experience;
- record-keeping systems are in place.

Figure 1.7 *Effective teaching and learning*

Most schools, when producing these checklists, firmly indicate that they are for guidance only, which at present follows the National Framework recommendations that: 'appraisal cannot and should not be designed to provide a simplified account of the appraisee's performance against a set of fixed criteria of good practice. We, therefore, strongly oppose the mechanistic use in appraisal of standard checklists of performance.'

Whichever format schools choose to use, it appears that the emphasis is moving in the direction of a more coherent professional criteria designed to improve the quality of both teaching and learning.

Following general self-appraisal the initial meeting takes place in which the appraisee can discuss ideas for a focus with the appraiser. It is always useful if the appraiser has been given an idea before the meeting so that they can have given some thought as to how they, as appraiser, will be able to help.

Self-appraisal for the appraisers should concentrate on what they can offer the appraisee. If the appraisee has given the appraiser an idea of their focus then it can be considered how best to help in this respect. The self-appraisal should concentrate on the skills which may be needed and how they can best be applied.

THE INITIAL MEETING

The purposes of the initial meeting have been described in many ways. The main ones, based on the National Framework and extended through experience, are summarised below:

- to confirm the purpose and clarify the context of the appraisal;
- to consider the teacher's job description;
- to agree the scope of the appraisal, in the context of school or departmental development plans;
- to agree the scope of the appraisal, identifying areas of the appraisee's job on which the appraisal might usefully focus;
- to agree the arrangements for, and the scope of, specific self-appraisal and its relationships to the other components of the programme;
- to agree arrangements for classroom observation, subject to the requirements of the scheme;
- to agree on the methods other than classroom observation by which data for the appraisal should be collected, subject to the requirements of the scheme;
- to agree a timetable for the appraisal process.

It is important for the success of the appraisal cycle that the appraisee and appraiser have a good professional relationship so that the appraisee feels confident about revealing possible areas of concern without being regarded as a poor teacher. A good relationship is important so that learning and development occur throughout the appraisal process. Chapter 5 looks at the personal skills needed and the awareness raising of staff necessary to conduct a valuable and developmental appraisal process. If the relationship lacks professional rigour the process becomes merely a 'back patting' exercise which will be meaningless and of little value to the teacher or the school.

It is interesting to look at what constitutes good relationships necessary to conduct an effective appraisal. The Regulations and Circular 12/91 assume that schools adopt a line management approach, believing, wherever possible, that a teacher's appraiser should be a 'person who already has management responsibility for him or her'. The ACAS report states that 'the appraiser of a teacher should be his or her immediate supervisor'. While many schools seem to follow this line management approach it does mean that responsibility remains within fairly rigidly defined curriculum areas. This fails to allow for the cross-fertilisation of both ideas and methods across the curriculum which lend themselves to much meaningful cross-curricular activity. Some schools have devised methods to allow cross-curricular appraisal systems to operate and feel that the benefits of observing the strengths and problems of other areas of the school provide a wider perspective to the participants, which has led to some interesting and valuable sharing of initiatives.

When the area of focus has been agreed it is useful for both participants to share information which may be helpful for the observation, collection of data and for the later interview or professional discussion. Curriculum vitae, job description, schemes of work, timetables or anything else that might be used to inform the process could be useful. It is also helpful in building good relationships if the participants share other information about themselves, such as background, experience and possible areas of knowledge about the focus. All these suggestions help to build an atmosphere of professional trust which will lead to a more productive and useful appraisal.

At the initial meeting, in addition to selecting and agreeing areas of focus and arranging the future timetable, it is necessary to agree the sources of appropriate information to be collected such as the documents that need to be read, the people that need to be consulted and the tasks to be observed. This information will normally be collected within half a term and the appraisal interview should take place as soon as possible after this process is finalised. All the information collected should be available to both the appraiser and the appraisee and no information received anonymously should be accepted.

The initial meeting and the appraisal interview both require time for the appraisee and appraiser to be together. This costs money and these meetings have to take place outside teaching contact time. In schools where all time is teacher contact, this proves very difficult and means before or after school meetings. Some schools soften this by paying for an off-site quiet, quality environment. This also helps to build good relationships between the appraisee and appraiser.

Obviously if the appraisee and appraiser continue to work together in the second cycle, the established relationship can be developed.

Specific self-appraisal

The more focused specific self-appraisal will take place after the initial meeting where the particular focus, or focuses, for this cycle has been discussed. Without the advantage of an individual general self-appraisal it is at this stage that the focuses can become imposed rather than negotiated. Having decided on the area of focus at an initial meeting, the specific self-appraisal can take place, providing an opportunity for more in-depth reflection on the focus and putting it into the context of the teacher's role in the school. As all areas of focus are highly individual, specific self-appraisal should necessarily reflect this and it is inappropriate to offer further prompt sheets.

During both processes of self-appraisal it is important for the appraisee to be honest but also to be fair. As a teacher it is all too easy to dwell on one's failures. The teaching profession has taken many knocks from outside sources in the past few years, coupled with an overload of new initiatives and National Curriculum directives, all of which initially led to the lowering of confidence and self-esteem within the profession. This then is a welcome opportunity to use time to dwell on strengths and achievements; on the successes rather than the failures. Declaring what we are good at, for adults, may feel culturally unacceptable; however, appraisees should not concentrate on being negatively self-critical, but develop the ability to acknowledge achievements. If the process of self-appraisal is to be valued and valuable, both to the individual and to the school, then an individual's strengths and capabilities should not be kept hidden. Only then can the appraisal system serve an individual in terms of staff development and career enhancement in a balanced way, and at the same time serve a school in terms of maximising the use of its most valuable resource: the teacher.

Some schools and LEAs take self-appraisal a step further and are beginning to evolve prompt sheets more in line with the competencies expected of newly qualified teachers. These schools would argue that it is difficult to appraise a teacher's effectiveness and the quality of the teaching and learning process in the classroom if you have not first set out to define the criteria against which to judge that effectiveness.

These schools produce more complicated prompt sheets rather than a simple prompt list for the appraisee to consider. These vary in form with some prompts examining the skills one possesses, prompting answers ranging from: comfortable with; fairly comfortable; less comfortable; to uncomfortable. Others list the characteristics they feel enhance effective teaching and learning and leave the individual to make a broad assessment of themselves. No doubt this is an area on which many battles are yet to be fought!

CLASSROOM OBSERVATION AND DATA COLLECTION

The ACAS report recommends that classroom observation should be the key element in the appraisal process as teaching is at the heart of the teacher's job. It has been this element of the appraisal cycle that appears to have threatened and worried teachers most. For years teachers have been able to close their classroom doors, build relationships with pupils and have a more or less autonomous professional existence. The introduction of appraisal, alongside the insistence on schemes of work coupled with notions of staff development linked to school development plans, and insistence on coherent monitoring and assessment procedures, has begun to change this perception. The introduction of the National Curriculum, with all its numerous modifications to digest, has added to the situation. Autonomy ends! Or does it?

All these initiatives are designed to make teachers more account-able and maybe the days of idiosyncratic teaching are over. What ought to result from a combination of these initiatives is a better-informed, better-trained teacher who is capable of making more effective decisions within the classroom to improve teaching and learning.

Teachers' main fear of the classroom observation component of appraisal seemed originally to rest on the assumption that not only would they lose their autonomy but that some form of a standard checklist approach would be introduced. At present a checklist approach to appraisal is only used for newly qualified teachers to help them at the self-appraisal stage. However, it could be that schools will want to come to some consensus about how they wish to improve teaching and learning across the curriculum and it may be beneficial to introduce some mechanism or performance indicator as an agreed school focus within the appraisal process.

The purpose of any classroom observation is to provide information about an aspect of work practice that will contribute to the professional discussion. The purpose and nature of the observation and the focus will have been decided at the initial meeting. The criteria and the method of observation to be used will also have been agreed beforehand. It is important that the activity to be observed has been agreed and is clear, manageable and realistic. If the observation is to play a useful role in the appraisal cycle observers must have a clear understanding of the context, the aims and the purposes of the lessons to be observed. This is where documentation relating to schemes of work and lesson plans are useful to the observer in placing this particular lesson in the more general context of teaching.

Decisions will also need to be considered about what to tell the pupils about observation. If the ethos of the school has traditionally been one of a closed-door policy then opening up classrooms can feel extremely threatening and any observation may well be perceived by both pupil and teacher as some form of disciplinary or inspection procedure. Careful attention must be paid to how the presence of an observer is explained to the pupils. In schools where there is a cross-curricular approach to appraisal rather than a line management model this problem is largely resolved. In such schools any suggestion of disciplinary or inspection elements in the observation are simply not an issue – the reverse seems to be the case. One school document, relating to its cross-curricular approach, stated that the observation component 'was, for most of the members, the most fascinating part of the process'. History teachers observing modern language lessons and science teachers looking at English lessons helped to create a deeper understanding of problems in different curriculum areas and helped relationships with students.

Using a cross-curricular model also makes it easier to explain to students that the observer in the classroom is there to learn about different teaching methods across the curriculum. This has the double bonus of making not only the teacher being observed the expert but also of raising the status of the pupils who feel that their contributions in the lesson are valued. This leaves the observer free to make as many notes as is necessary and practical. In primary schools it may be that this approach necessarily almost happens by default, whereas special schools are able to make their own arrangements based on their particular strengths.

It is difficult in many classroom situations for the observer to remain unobtrusive. Some teachers may prefer the observer to be involved with the pupils or the lessons but it needs to be recognised that this approach may affect the observation task and change both the nature and the quality of the observation and the data collected. It is imperative that the observer is unrestricted to record what it is that has actually been accurately observed, based not on assumptions and expectations of performance but on objective and constructive concentration.

Note taking may not be the method decided on to record the observation, but whatever method is used must have been clearly understood and agreed upon beforehand, making use of evidence and not judgement. It may be appropriate to use an observation recording form of some description. Many authorities and schools design their own while others use one already in existence.

Figures 1.8–1.10 are examples of such forms.

Prompt List

It must be stressed that this list is neither prescriptive nor exhaustive and may need modification in the light of experience gained during the Pilot Study.

A. The Teacher in the Classroom

Preparation The activity was part of a properly planned programme.
      The aim of the activity was clear.
      A suitable approach was chosen from the options available.
      Adequate and suitable resources were available.
      The learning environment had been considered.

Teaching skills: The material was well presented.
      The pupils were actively involved.
      The teacher adapted the approach when necessary:
      – was aware of individual needs within the group.
      – displayed mastery of the subject matter.

Follow-up: Homework is regularly set (if appropriate).
      Pupils' work is marked and recorded regularly.
      Pupils receive appropriate feedback about their work.
      Parents are informed of pupils' work and progress in accordance with school policy.
      The teacher evaluates the success of his/her teaching.

B. The Teacher in the School and the Community

Care for   The teacher is involved in the pastoral curriculum:
individual pupil: – actively furthers the discipline and aims of the school;
      – seeks, in appropriate cases, to liaise with outside agencies, ie EWO, psychologist, etc.

(School Teacher Appraisal: A National Framework HMSO, 1989)

Figure 1.8 *Prompt list*

Classroom Observation Recording Sheet

Date of observation: **Duration:** *60 minutes*

Focus: *Classroom Organisation and Management*   **Group/Class:** *R/Y1*

Agreed criteria to be observed: – *Opportunities for teacher to focus on small group teaching*
                                        – *Time on task when children not supervised by teacher*
                                        – *Opportunities for children to work independently and collaboratively without teacher direction*

LESSON DEVELOPMENT	DATA FOR DISCUSSION
Children return from assembly. Meet on carpet area. Teacher explained work to be covered by all children and the learning demands for each area of the classroom.	*Teacher gave children opportunity to discuss their first choice of activity and who they would be working with. Some children appear uncertain but majority of children set off to select their tasks. Children respect rules about numbers of children able to use each area.*
Teacher informed those children she wished to work with her. Asked these children to meet in book area while teacher helped other children to set about tasks.	*Children gathered in book area. Certain amount of jostling as they look for space. Children wait for ten minutes as teacher set other children to work and answered queries. Children actively engaged in water play and construction area. Boys dominate home play. Some children not sure what to do and approach teacher. Teacher directs children and they settle quickly.*
Teacher sat with small group. Storying activity.	*Two children want to make a book. Stapler is jammed. Approached to resolve situation. Teacher fixes stapler. Teacher works with small group.*
Teacher calls all children to carpet area for story before playtime.	*Shrieks from painting area. Spillage of black paint. Children gather to watch. Teacher leaves small group to mop up mess. No mop. Teacher uses newspaper.*

Figure 1.9 *Example of a classroom observation recording sheet*

Classroom Observation Recording Sheet

Date of observation: *23 September 10.00am–11.00am* **Duration:** *60 minutes*

Focus: *Teaching and Learning Strategies* **Group/Class:** *Year 9*

Agreed criteria to be observed: – *Delivery of instructions/information*
– *Questioning techniques*
– *Opportunities for children to work independently*

LESSON DEVELOPMENT	DATA FOR DISCUSSION
Topic introduced by teacher.	*Information given explaining subject – specific terminology. Attempt to build on prior knowledge with reference to a previous visit to the Roman Wall.*
Teacher instructed whole group re task.	*After instructions were given three boys and two girls asked for more clarification on what they were meant to be doing.*
Whole class read silently.	*No pupil asked for clarification of the text. Later one girl and one boy intimated that they did not understand what they had read.*
Teacher questioned pupils on text.	*Six out of ten questions received one-word answers.* *Two questions were answered by teacher.* *Two developed thinking.*
Teacher divided class into four groups and gave more detailed instructions of their tasks.	*Two groups coped well with this – they seemed to be enthusiastic and well motivated. One group monopolised the teacher for the entire activity. One group sharpened pencils, gossiped about a TV programme and in response to the question 'Why don't you begin the task?' answered they did not know what they were meant to do.*
Pupils worked in groups of seven on tasks.	*The outcomes for all group activities was a piece of imaginative writing.*
Work was collected for marking.	*Feedback on work was promised for next lesson.*

Figure 1.10 *Example of classroom observation recording sheet*

After the observation the observer should provide some immediate, if brief, informal feedback, say within two days of the observation. The initial feedback avoids leaving the teacher in any prolonged state of nervous apprehension and gives an opportunity to comment on the activity while the memory is still fresh. It is important to bear in mind that this debriefing should not only be supportive but also developmental. The feedback should be constructive and based only on the evidence of the observation, and comments should only be made on behaviour that can be changed. Space should be allowed for the appraisee to offer their perceptions of the lesson observed. Recognition and celebration of the strengths of the appraisee and the achievements of the lesson should be made while offering alternative suggestions, or at least providing an opportunity for alternatives to be explored, if this is appropriate. In order to achieve this it is far more productive to be descriptive rather than judgemental.

Use the 'POD' framework to check that:

1. The *planning* has been adequate. This applies to both the appraiser and the appraisee.
2. The agreed criteria have been followed for the *observation*.
3. There has been adequate *discussion*, both at the initial meeting and in the short feedback immediately following the observation.

Although classroom observation is seen to be the key part in the process of gathering information the selection of areas of focus for appraisal may take into account other aspects of a teacher's job description as well as school and departmental development plans. As already mentioned, classroom observation is compulsory in teacher appraisal. Headteachers may be observed performing other duties which becomes task observation, but at present they are the only people who can work on this in place of classroom observation. Teachers may have task as well as classroom observation if they agree this with the appraiser. The vast majority of teachers, in addition to teaching, will have other areas of responsibility which might include pastoral or administrative aspects relating to the curriculum or other school activities or initiatives. It will be necessary, therefore, to collect information about the exercise of these responsibilities outside the classroom. It is essential that the collection of information related to these other activities be handled with sensitivity.

Data collection

At the initial meeting the appraiser should agree with the appraisee what information it would be appropriate to collect, from what sources and by what methods. Information for data collection may come from paper sources in the form of records, reports, plans etc, or it may be communicated by others. Before collecting data from other people it is advisable to be familiar with the Code of Practice (Annex A – DfE Circular 12/91) regarding the ethics and procedures for data collection. When collecting data from other people it is advisable not to seek personal opinion but to try to ensure that all information is both sought and presented in an objective way. This allows those giving information to make fair and considered contributions which they are prepared to substantiate with evidence if required. Any general comment should be supported with specific evidence.

THE APPRAISAL INTERVIEW

This component of the appraisal cycle is often referred to as the 'professional discussion', perhaps a warmer name than 'interview'. Whatever the terminology used, an extended discussion between the appraiser and the appraisee is an essential and compulsory component of any appraisal scheme.

During this process successes are identified and any developmental or training needs are agreed. At this stage professional targets for future action are set. These targets must be precise, realistic and capable of being monitored, whether they relate to individual needs or to the needs of the school. In terms of monitoring, targets need to be precise as it is very difficult to conceive of performance indicators that can usefully be applied to vague notions of harder work or improved motivation. Ensure that when you set targets they are SMART:

- Specific
- Measurable
- Achievable
- Realistic
- Time bound.

The appraisal interview should provide an opportunity for genuine dialogue and must take place without interruptions. This is why many schools have chosen to make use of some of the professional development days for appraisal interviews. This assists in achieving both uninterrupted time and an easing of the financial constraints to already overstretched budgets. The following headings may be useful to help record the interview:

- Teaching Activity Planning and Preparation
- Classroom Observation and Management
- Teaching Skills
- Relationships.

Some schools suggest a more general agenda with topics covering the teacher in the classroom, the school and the community, while others broaden the areas to cover management roles, where appropriate. Some schools have suggested topics to be covered which follow similar headings to those used by the government in producing their list of competencies for newly qualified teachers.

The appraisal interview provides an opportunity to discuss the agreed areas of the teacher's work, while giving feedback and recognition on the basis of the classroom observation and the data collected. It assists the appraisee to identify areas of professional and career development and it provides the forum to negotiate targets for that development. It also provides information for negotiating the writing of the statement. During the interview it may be necessary to discuss and modify the appraisee's job description in conjunction with discussing appropriate career development.

The interview provides the opportunity to negotiate and clarify points that are to be included in the appraisal statement. In order to ensure confidentiality it is recommended that, once agreement has been reached on the content of this statement, the appraiser writes it in person. This avoids any chance that the written statement lies around waiting to be typed. The statement may be compiled and written during the interview process. There is no suggestion that every word spoken in the discussion should be recorded as the purpose of the statement is to provide a summary of the main focus of the appraisal discussion. Many schools have a standard recording sheet for both the targets set and the appraisal statement. An example of each is included (see Figures 1.11 and 1.12).

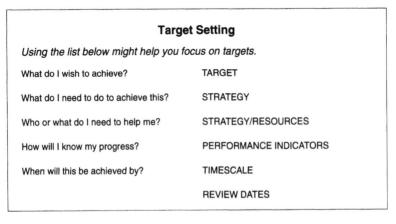

Target Setting

Using the list below might help you focus on targets.

What do I wish to achieve?	TARGET
What do I need to do to achieve this?	STRATEGY
Who or what do I need to help me?	STRATEGY/RESOURCES
How will I know my progress?	PERFORMANCE INDICATORS
When will this be achieved by?	TIMESCALE
	REVIEW DATES

Figure 1.11 *Target setting*

Teacher Appraisal Statement

Appraisee: _____

Appraiser: _____

Date of Appraisal Interview: _____

Summary of Appraisal Interview

This should include a brief record of the main points discussed, the conclusion reached and the professional development targets agreed.

Signature of appraiser: _____ Date: _____

Comment by appraisee: _____
(This section does not have to be filled in)

_____

_____

Signature of appraisee: _____

Signature of appraiser: _____

Figure 1.12 *Teacher appraisal statement*

The appraisee has the right to add a comment to the appraisal statement if they wish. While this remains an undisputed right, if it is insisted upon it may be implicit that there has been some degree of dissatisfaction with the process and the final statement that has emerged, though this should not necessarily be the case. Every effort should be made to avoid this outcome. Relationship building and skills training will greatly reduce the likelihood of such occurrences.

Another question that frequently worries teachers relates to the ownership of and access to the final appraisal statement. Paragraph 57 DfE (DfEE) Circular 12/91 states that 'Documents produced during an appraisal, other than the appraisal statement, should be destroyed once the statement has been finalised.' This safeguards any careless handling of the considerable data collected during the information gathering section of the appraisal cycle.

Appraisal statements are personal documents of a particularly sensitive kind and should, therefore, be treated carefully and kept in a secure place. Access to the statement should be restricted to the appraiser, appraisee and headteacher. Access to the targets set, however, needs to be wider. This is where information for school and individual developmental needs is formulated. For the school to plan its budget and prioritise those identified needs, it is necessary that the information relating to those targets is available to the person responsible for staff and school development planning. This point is reinforced by Regulation 14(2): 'Those responsible for planning the training and development of school teachers in a school (including, in the case of a school maintained by a local education authority, appropriate officers of or advisers to that authority) shall receive particulars of any targets for action relating to training and development.' Governors do not a have a right of access to statements but do have a right of access to appraisal targets on request. In many LEAs this has been done on a non-attributable, aggregated basis.

After the statement and targets have been produced there should be semi-formal meetings to monitor progress of the targets set. This will happen between the statement being written and the formal review meeting that takes place during the second year of the cycle.

FOLLOW-UP REVIEW MEETING

This meeting can be as long or as short as is necessary, bearing in mind the relationships established and the time and financial constraints on school budgets. It does need to be formalised by agreeing a time and place, however, otherwise it can appear casual and undervalued. The follow-up review is then seen to be providing a formal opportunity to enhance the professional relationship developed between appraiser and appraisee. It is important to review the progress made towards achieving the targets that were set out at the appraisal interview and outlined as part of the appraisal statement, as it may be necessary to modify or alter the targets, for reasons of both time and experience. This discussion also allows time to begin to prepare and think about the next appraisal cycle.

The management of the appraisal cycle may appear to be rather daunting in terms of both time and finance. However, we have pointed to a few ideas that make it possible to produce benefits, both to the individual and to the school. A system that firmly links appraisal with school development plans and initiatives that are perceived as priorities, either by the school or from the demands of an OFSTED inspection, can result in improvements all round, but only if there is the will to bring this about. What better way to link development and resources than using the appraisal system as a key element to future development plans?

The benefits to the school or institution are manifold. The appraisal cycle provides more accurate information about teacher performance and developmental needs, while giving opportunities to improve that performance in the process of target setting. Improved communication and relationship building, including networking, are obvious. The appraisal system offers an excellent opportunity for the identification and coordination of staff and school developmental needs, which in turn can offer an avenue of communication to clarify the aims and objectives across the whole school. All these aspects enrich the learning environment of the school by enhancing both teaching and learning methods.

The benefits to the individual teacher in terms of recognition of skills and expertise and in the identification and support for staff development should raise morale and, by definition, raise standards. This cannot be taken for granted as it involves the need for motivation and for results to be seen. Increased job satisfaction should follow through discussion of work and career development in a supportive environment. This will lead to an increased involvement, not only in immediate considerations of individual classroom management and skills, but to an understanding of a wider perspective of whole school management and development policies. This should then lead to an understanding as to how the individual fits into that wider philosophy and foster a sense of community and commitment rather than the apparent comfort of isolation. This increased self-confidence and awareness can only benefit the school by contributing considerably to overall school improvement in terms of raising professionalism and thereby improving both teaching and learning across the curriculum.

After the review meeting, the appraisee and appraiser should look to the future and discuss how to improve the process. The next section may help.

A FUTURE PERSPECTIVE

The Cinderella of the appraisal process has always been the data collection aspect. Unlike observation this has been optional, perhaps not quite seen as an optional *extra*, but nonetheless an option. Consequently it has been used in some appraisals but not the majority. There are two main reasons for this:

1. In the early days of appraisal data collection was greeted with suspicion, scepticism and apprehension. The summer of 1991, when the appraisal Regulations appeared, saw some sections of the press seizing on possibilities of parents being asked to score teacher performance, Torvill and Dean style, at the school gates, or courses being offered to appraisers in how to use leading questions on unsuspecting governors or children. This was despite the fact that a strong Code of Practice had been issued to ensure that data collection was a positive, professional process.
2. Where data collection has been used, mainly with headteachers, it has invariably proved very time consuming. In some cases those involved felt the time to be very well spent and beneficial, but nevertheless the time has to be found from somewhere.

Recently the concept of so-called 360° appraisal has been interesting the human resource departments of both manufacturing and service industries. This idea, when presented to a group of teachers as the way in which a large insurance group was moving, was greeted with the comment, 'You have seen the future!' Our own reaction was that the teacher appraisal scheme has always seen the future, but has somehow missed connecting it to the present. The appraisal Regulations have always contained the essential base elements of 360° appraisal, though they have never been fully exploited. Maybe now at this crossroads time for appraisal we need to take another look at how it is conducted, before the commercial world takes all the credit.

So what is 360° appraisal? No doubt the staffroom jokes about going round in circles could fill several break times! It is a performance measuring tool which is used to identify how well people are doing in their jobs and what development and training needs would help in the future. In place of the traditional one- or two-dimensional appraisal process, where the appraisal is a mixture of line management and self-appraisal, 360° gives the opportunity for all who have an involvement in a person's performance to comment and give feedback. In this way those who are best qualified to comment are able to do so from their direct observations of the person at work. Information can be collected by questionnaire and interview. This is usually done on paper but, providing confidentiality can be assured, why not use electronic means, for example tape recording or computers?

Once information is collected and collated it is fed back by the appraiser to the appraisee in a skilful way. Some benefits claimed for 360° are that:

- It can motivate, because people see information coming from those with whom they interact in a wide aspect of their job rather than the potentially restricted view of one appraiser.
- It may prove fairer than other means of information collection because the same information is sought from a wide range of people.
- It may be less time consuming than periods of observation.
- It involves a range of people who have the ability to describe the evidence rather than give a potentially subjective viewpoint from one or two specific observations.
- It provides meaningful feedback on performance, leading to celebration and improvement.

If this is increasingly working in industrial settings, why not in teacher appraisal, which clearly already contains the essence of the 360° structure in data collection? There may be those who recoil from the statement that appraisal may be seen as a performance measuring tool, stating that it is about personal and professional development. We would not argue, but without a measure of current performance how can high levels be celebrated and areas for development be identified? How can continuous improvements be recorded and communicated and, perhaps more importantly, linked to improvements in teaching and learning for *all* in schools? Surely the questions are really about who is doing the measuring, what are the measures being used for and how are the measures being made?

In the 360° model the measurements can be decided on the basis of what is needed for the employee to carry out their job effectively and efficiently to meet the objectives of the business. Increasingly, in those organisations involved in continuous improvement, this information is driven by the employee, who is kept fully informed of what the business objectives are and what progress is being made towards achieving them. There is also a recognition that part of the motivation for employees comes from their having the freedom and encouragement for self-development, that is, development not always directly business related. Is there really a difference between this and what exists in those schools striving for continuous improvement? We think not.

We believe that the future of appraisal in teaching depends on a number of reinforcements being made to what is current best practice. If such reinforcements are made then 360° appraisal can become a reality, involving teachers in less effort and producing more effective results than at present.

The appraisal of teachers and all other members of staff has to have a direct and positively focused link to the performance of their day-to-day activities in the school and how this relates to the work of the department and/or school as a whole. This needs accurate feedback from those involved. Therefore we advocate greater use of the data collection part of appraisal in order to do this. Data collection from a range of people connected with the teacher's job can provide powerful and rigorous feedback. Under 360° principles people use their continuous observations to feed back information.

To make the system work effectively and within equality of opportunity, an agreed whole school or departmental questionnaire could be drawn up with certain base questions. These would relate to how the appraisee performs in her or his job as seen by the person answering the questions. Additional questions specifically agreed between appraisee and appraiser could then be added.

At present, under the Circular 12/91 Code of Practice, all information gathered is open, including the name of the provider of the information. In some 360° schemes names are confidential, and perhaps more debate is needed on this point.

However appraisees and appraisers should be encouraged to use information from all those with whom the teacher interacts – in short encouraging a 360° rather than the 90° or 180° view currently in use.

2

Evaluating the Effectiveness of Appraisal

This chapter is based on research carried out over three years and covering a number of geographical areas. Our initial research was conducted in a large LEA with a mixture of urban and rural schools. This LEA scheme for teacher and headteacher appraisal emphasises that appraisal is a developmental, continuous and systematic process intended to assist teachers in their professional development and career planning. During our evaluation the LEA saw the need for their scheme to be developed from the experience and perceptions of those who had already been involved in the process. This was particularly relevant as the Regulations require all teachers and head-teachers for whom the LEA are responsible to have been appraised, at least once, by 1995. The evaluation would then be used to inform future practice and ensure appraisal continued to be treated as a dynamic process, subject to modification and development in order to achieve maximum effectiveness.

We choose to use the findings of this research, together with our later research, as we feel it to be of importance in highlighting certain trends, which have now become even more urgent. One of the stated, or implicit aims of many schemes is that appraisal is a dynamic process subject to modification and development. The operative words here appear to be the recognition of the need for modification and development of appraisal schemes to gain the maximum use of time and resources, both human and financial, for the benefit of the school and ultimately the pupils.

In many schools the main findings show that the formal structures required to link all aspects of school development planning – OFSTED inspections, appraisal and National Curriculum accountability – in a manageable and potentially beneficial way have yet to be developed.

Appraisal Evaluation

Response Form

Please answer all questions. Tick the space which best reflects your response to each statement.

In my own experience as an appraisee, the appraisal process has:

	Yes	No
1. helped me to improve my skills in the areas of focus	☐	☐
2. led to greater recognition of my achievements (in at least one area)	☐	☐
3. helped me to identify my training needs	☐	☐
4. led to further training	☐	☐
5. led to a change/changes in my duties/responsibilities	☐	☐
6. led to changes in my job description	☐	☐
7. enhanced my career prospects	☐	☐
8. changed my classroom practice	☐	☐
9. operated fairly in terms of equality of opportunity	☐	☐
10. made me feel that any reference written for me would be more accurate	☐	☐

	Very effective	Effective	Fairly effective	Ineffective
11. The introduction of appraisal in my school has been				
12. The influence of the appraisal process on school development planning has been				
13. In improving the quality of education for pupils, the appraisal process has been				
14. In achieving the DfE's stated aims of improving the management of a school, the appraisal process has been				
15. In terms of achieving a sensitive match between appraisers and appraisees, the appraisal process has been				

	Very useful	Useful	Fairly useful	Not very useful
16. As an appraisee, I have found the process				
17. As an appraiser, I have found the process				

18. Which parts of the process, if any, do you feel were beneficial to you
(please tick as appropriate)

Self-appraisal	☐	Data collection	☐
Interview	☐	Initial meeting	☐
Statement writing and target setting	☐	Observation	☐

Please use the reverse side of this page if there are further comments you wish to make about the implementation or outcomes of the appraisal process.

Figure 2.1 *Example of appraisal evaluation form*

Appraisal Evaluation

Response Form

Please answer all questions. Tick the space which best reflects your response to each statement.

In my own experience as an appraisee, the appraisal process has:

	Yes	No
1. helped me to improve my skills in the areas of focus	55%	45%
2. led to greater recognition of my achievements (in at least one area)	64%	36%
3. helped me to identify my training needs	56%	44%
4. led to further training	13%	87%
5. led to a change/changes in my duties/responsibilities	14%	86%
6. led to changes in my job description	18%	82%
7. enhanced my career prospects	8%	92%
8. changed my classroom practice	45%	55%
9. operated fairly in terms of equality of opportunity	84%	16%
10. made me feel that any reference written for me would be more accurate	37%	63%

	Very effective	Effective	Fairly effective	Ineffective
11. The introduction of appraisal in my school has been	5%	39%	47%	9%
12. The influence of the appraisal process on school development planning has been	1%	29%	43%	27%
13. In improving the quality of education for pupils, the appraisal process has been	0%	29%	42%	29%
14. In achieving the DfE's stated aims of improving the management of a school, the appraisal process has been	0%	25%	42%	33%
15. In terms of achieving a sensitive match between appraisers and appraisees, the appraisal process has been	30%	40%	25%	5%

	Very useful	Useful	Fairly useful	Not very useful
16. As an appraisee, I have found the process	8%	42%	25%	25%
17. As an appraiser, I have found the process	21%	37%	23%	19%

18. Which parts of the process, if any, do you feel were beneficial to you
    (please tick as appropriate)

Self-appraisal	62%	Data collection	21%
Interview	39%	Initial meeting	17%
Statement writing and target setting	28%	Observation	38%

Please use the reverse side of this page if there are further comments you wish to make about the implementation of the appraisal process.

Figure 2.2 *Example of appraisal evaluation form with eventual findings*

Appraisal Evaluation

Response Form

Please answer all questions. Tick the space which best reflects your response to each statement.

In my own experience as an appraisee, the appraisal process has:

	Yes	No
1. helped me to improve my skills in the areas of focus	65%	35%
2. led to greater recognition of my achievements (in at least one area)	60%	40%
3. helped me to identify my training needs	54%	46%
4. led to further training	17%	83%
5. led to a change/changes in my duties/responsibilities	13%	87%
6. led to changes in my job description	7%	93%
7. enhanced my career prospects	12%	88%
8. changed my classroom practice	38%	62%
9. operated fairly in terms of equality of opportunity	85%	15%

	Very effective	Effective	Fairly effective	Ineffective
10. The introduction of appraisal in my school has been	7%	38%	38%	17%
11. The influence of the appraisal process on school development planning has been	2%	20%	42%	36%
12. In improving the quality of education for pupils, the appraisal process has been	4%	20%	38%	32%
13. In achieving the DfE's stated aims of improving the management of a school, the appraisal process has been	3%	25%	38%	32%
14. In terms of achieving a sensitive match between appraisers and appraisees, the appraisal process has been	33%	40%	20%	7%

	Very useful	Useful	Fairly useful	Not very useful
15. As an appraisee, I have found the process	15%	32%	27%	26%
16. As an appraiser, I have found the process	21%	36%	27%	16%

17. Which timescale most closely matches that in which you completed your appraisal as an appraisee?	More than one term	32%	Half a term	24%
	One term	21%	Less than half a term	23%

18. Approximately how many hours in total did each appraisal take you:

    (a) as an appraisee 3 hours (to the nearest hour)

    (b) as an appraiser 5 hours (to the nearest hour)

19. Please use the reverse side of this page if there are further comments you wish to make about the implementation or outcomes of the appraisal process.

Figure 2.3 *Example of appraisal evaluation form with eventual findings*

THE EVALUATION PROCESS

A general response form (see Figure 2.1) was given to every member of staff in the schools taking part. Using a tick-sheet format, its purpose was to provide a profile of respondents' experiences and perceptions of appraisal. A statistical breakdown of the responses received (varying from 10 per cent to, in one case, 100 per cent of a captive audience) can be seen in Figures 2.2 and 2.3. Respondents were also invited to write comments about the implementation or outcomes of the appraisal process. These responses were considered alongside those to the second questionnaire, which took the form of interview questions (see Figure 2.4). The selection of schools was balanced to represent all phases. All respondents were given the option of confidentiality. Their responses have provided first-hand evidence of issues arising from, or affecting, appraisal and are the focus of this chapter.

1 What aspects of the appraisal process did you find useful personally or professionally?

Responses to this question ranged over positive aspects of the whole appraisal process. Many teachers believed that it provided an opportunity to enhance and build relationships and this aspect of relationship building was highlighted in all schools. Appraisal was seen as useful as it confirmed impressions of teachers' individual strengths, offering a chance to show their skills and commitment. It was seen by most as a positive, non-threatening experience that reinforced sound practice and supported change.

In most primary schools appraisal was seen as an excellent tool for creating a positive atmosphere of trust and well-being. It was seen, across all phases, as an opportunity to share concerns and discuss topics and proved a mechanism for a formal recognition and acknowledgement of a teacher's strengths and achievements.

Self-appraisal provided time and space to sit and reflect. In schools where the headteacher, as well as the appraiser, found time to have a follow-up discussion, staff felt even more that their strengths had been recognised and valued.

Where cross-curricular models of appraisal had been adopted staff valued not only the cross-fertilisation of ideas but the realisation that they also often shared the same problems. Comments ranged from: 'Personally and professionally I enjoyed working with another curriculum area and with a colleague who normally I would have little contact with' to 'It was really interesting to look in depth at the work of another department and to feel that I was able to make some constructive contribution to take them forward.' Where those interviewed acted as both appraiser and appraisee several responses indicated an awareness of the transferable nature of the listening and interviewing skills acquired in training for appraisal.

2 What aspects of the appraisal process did you find not particularly useful to you personally or professionally?

Many of the concerns expressed were shared by appraisers and appraisees alike. In spite of the difficulties identified many had

---

Appraisal Evaluation – Interview Questions

The appraisal process:

1. What aspects of the appraisal process did you find useful personally or professionally?
2. What aspects of the appraisal process did you find not particularly useful personally or professionally?

After the statement was written:

3. In what ways, if any, do you feel your skills and achievements have received greater recognition since your involvement in the appraisal process?
4. In what ways, if any, have your job description or your duties changed as a result of the appraisal process?
5. In what ways, if any, has the appraisal process helped you in terms of your professional development?
6. Do you think your career prospects might have been enhanced by the appraisal process? If so, how?
7. What changes, if any, have you made to your classroom practice as a result of the appraisal process?
8. If the appraisal process indicated/identified in-service needs for your professional development, how are these being met/likely to be met, for example:
   (a) school-based support/INSET;
   (b) higher education institutions;
   (c) LEA INSET;
   (d) other – please describe briefly.
9. What contribution, if any, do you think the appraisal process generally has made/will make to:
   (a) school development planning;
   (b) improving the quality of education for pupils;
   (c) more effective school management.

Figure 2.4 *Appraisal evaluation – interview questions*

overcome them. For others, the difficulties seemed beyond their own control and they remained disappointed with the outcome.

Time factors were a major issue discussed in all the research. Some resented time away from their own classroom, others felt there was lack of depth due to the pressures of time, and that appraisal provided only a 'snapshot', while others felt that time constraints imposed on professional interviews devalued the experience, feeling that it was all too rushed or often subject to interruptions. The time between the observation and the interview for some was too long; they complained of loss of momentum or changes in the context of the school invalidating the process or preventing targets being met. Others saw appraisal as 'yet another thing to be done', but admitted that they used the time to indulge in 'a mutual whingeing session'.

Many appraisees' difficulties centred on their ability to select an appropriate focus that was both manageable and observable. Many felt that there was a strong argument to feed into the appraisal system not only a mechanism for providing an opportunity for the setting of individual focuses but also for the setting of focuses relating to the school's priorities and the departmental needs. In schools where the targets were fed into a systematic approach to staff development there was little frustration in the area of meeting targets or complaints about realising expectations. However, many felt that one of the weaknesses of the appraisal system as a mechanism for a coherent staff development policy was directly attributable to the confidential nature of the target setting, feeling that their statement sat in a drawer and was not followed up. Others felt frustration that although their concerns had been clearly identified and accepted as valid nothing had been done to address them. This dissatisfaction was often related to the position of the appraiser in the hierarchy. It was often perceived that the higher the prestige of the appraiser the higher in the line of priorities went the targets of the appraisee.

Another area of concern highlighted was that the monitoring that takes place during appraisal focuses on the individual, but it needs to focus on the school as well. This was particularly relevant in Cumbria where, during their national pilot, schools identified the needs of the school before focusing on the needs of the individual. Many felt that this rigour had been lost and that appraisal had become too cosy and comfortable. Not only did it have no teeth, but its gums were not even hard. Schools with this viewpoint could argue that the whole school staff need to arrive at a set of agreed criteria by which to judge the effectiveness of a teacher. They argued that just as students were given clear targets resulting in an honest dialogue for helping them achieve, the same should be expected from teachers.

Performance monitoring was seen in this context as a good thing, but it needed to be focused from the school's perspective and within the context of an agreed ethos, and then fed into the appropriate system.

Following on from this position, it was felt that in the area of target setting (and the very personal and, therefore, *ad hoc* nature of setting targets) the mechanism of appraisal often wastes an excellent opportunity to benefit both the school and the individual by not making the targets more public. Many suggested moving from a predominantly individual perspective to a whole school perspective.

3 In what ways do you feel your skills and achievements have received greater recognition?

A recurring feature in all the responses was that of raised awareness of the teacher's own skills as a result of the appraisal process, from generally feeling more confident to a feeling that the process led to an affirmation of self-worth. Most felt that it accentuated the positive, but because of this some felt that appraisal had too soft an edge. This was felt, in some cases, to be positive as it reinforced the feel good factor but others expressed dissatisfaction, as appraisal was not there to solve problems but to help people face reality.

A recognition of skills by colleagues was welcomed and in all cases led to enhanced relationships between appraiser and appraisee and often, where a separate follow-up meeting was arranged, with the headteacher. Where this follow-up did not happen there was a fear that the statements were not acknowledged, and some felt that they were not even read. These individuals feared that their statements simply disappeared into a dark hole.

Although many of those interviewed believed that the recognition of skills was restricted to the appraiser/appraisee by the confidential nature of the process, some reported a direct link to the appraisal process and promotion. Examples of this ranged from a head of Biology being promoted to head of Science, a teacher rising from a Scale A post through to Scale C, and another teacher becoming a project team leader for human resources in the school, again as a direct result of the individual wishing for greater involvement in whole school issues.

The confidentiality of the statement was seen by many to be a disadvantage. Many of those interviewed believed that this aspect of appraisal should perhaps not be taken so literally and that the targets should be passed, at the very least, to the staff development officer. It was suggested that unless this happened it was doubtful if individual targets would be met. Where there was no coordination of targets the most efficient use of school resources may not be made.

4 In what ways, if any, have your job description or your duties changed?

Apart from those promotions or recognition of skills already noted in the previous answers, only a few people reported significant changes as a direct result of appraisal. Several respondents reported a change in job description through their own initiative, where they voluntarily took on more responsibilities.

However, two people reported changes in the job descriptions related to a department or area of responsibility as a direct result of discussion during the appraisal interviews. In one case the changes related to technicians having their job descriptions simplified into an all-embracing general specification, rather than a specific area-related description. In another curriculum area it was accepted that extra-curricular work for part-time members of the department was on a voluntary basis rather than, as had previously been expected, a compulsory element in the job of drama teachers in that school.

5 In what ways has the appraisal process helped you?

Many of the aspects of professional development identified were related to an individual's area of focus. Replies ranged from improved organisation and time management, a more varied approach to teaching strategies, an improved ability to differentiate in terms of mixed ability teaching, to sharing ideas and looking at new teaching methods.

Many replies indicated more all-embracing aspects of enhanced professional development, reflecting changes in relationships, attitudes and understanding. Many replies indicated that individuals no longer felt isolated, and that as a result of the process they had a greater awareness of a whole school perspective rather than a collection of individuals. These responses included recognising a greater sympathy to other people's perspectives, enhanced relationships with other teachers, and a feeling of belonging to a particular school and knowing how they fitted in.

In schools where there was a coherent structure for staff development and appraisal many of those interviewed stressed the importance of appraisal as an instrument for not only identifying their individual strengths, but for enabling them to use those strengths to enhance their professional development. This was as well as using them for the benefit of teams, year groups, departments or the whole school. Respondents reported that when they had been invited to provide whole school INSET they learned a lot about how to approach and deliver it. The school benefited from utilising that person's expertise and the individual benefited by being involved in training, itself a strong personal development. The most useful example was given by a recently appointed librarian in Newcastle who was anxious to become involved with all departments and pupils to develop IT skills in desktop publishing and multimedia. An audit of department needs had immediately been set in motion as a direct result of the appraisal interview, with obvious benefits to the school following from this.

6 Do you think that your career prospects might have been enhanced by the appraisal process?

Relatively few respondents overall considered that their career prospects might have been enhanced directly as a result of the appraisal cycle, except those referred to in response to Question 3. Many teachers, however, felt that their references would be informed by the appraisal statement and would be accurate and positive. Many felt they had gained in confidence and had an improved awareness of their personal strengths through appraisal. This was attributed to the shared feel good factor that the process promoted.

7 What changes have you made to your classroom practice?

A significant number of teachers felt that the demands of the National Curriculum had forced changes in teaching styles in order to deliver the Key Stages, and that their changing classroom practices were more attributable to those forces than to the appraisal process. Others felt that the preparation for, and follow-up from, the OFSTED inspection had served as a greater motivator for change than the individual appraisal process. However, in schools where appraisal had been a positive, well-managed experience, most teachers were able to identify specific changes to classroom practice.

There was a great deal of reference to the modification of work sheets in recognition of the need for differentiation. Teachers comments varied. There were references to a broadening of teaching styles, varying the tasks in any particular lesson or adopting a different approach to group work.

Many felt that since appraisal they had more confidence to tackle the problems of mixed ability teaching by having small mixed ability groups within a larger framework or changing seating arrangements as a device for defusing potentially disruptive behaviour. Most recognised the need to adapt material to suit the needs of the pupils at whatever level of ability they were operating. At one end of the spectrum comments were received about raised expectations while another teacher was delighting in the new-found confidence and freedom of simply talking to the pupils and worrying less about the mountains of written outcomes. This is the area where the greatest potential for the future development of appraisal lies.

Other teachers referred to organising practical lessons from a central position rather than delivering from the front as had been their custom. Clearer instructions, delivery and explanations were other changes made in the classroom. Many felt more confident in giving pupils independence in the classroom as they now felt able to stand back as the pupils worked at the task set.

In schools where appraisal had been devalued, was viewed as a bolt-on initiative and seen as yet another chore to be done, teachers saw little connection between the appraisal process and the raising of standards, nor did they view it as a mechanism for change. In some cases the focus had been too broad, time management in the appraisal poor and momentum was lost, or follow-up and help to achieve targets had not been forthcoming. These factors seem to have led to negative responses and little awareness of any value to be gleaned from the process.

8 If the appraisal process indicated/identified in-service needs for your professional development, how are these being met/ likely to be met?

(a) School-based support/INSET
In a large number of cases teachers referred to their needs being met through their own efforts or with support within the school. Ideas for meeting the needs within the school demonstrated a variety of strategies and considerable imaginative use of time.

Teachers often observed other teachers, especially where techniques were being used which they felt could apply to their lessons. In one school the drama teacher was much in demand as a resource where the techniques were seen to be useful across the curriculum. This led to a slight overload on that department's time so a slot – on a training day – was arranged to cater for more staff together. In another secondary school a weekly twilight session was arranged for the languages department to share its ideas as an active form of staff development. A further junior school headteacher had used many imaginative and innovative methods of staff development, including the use of circus or roundabout sessions where the pupils move to teachers with different expertise enabling other members of staff either to observe or to participate when they felt confident. Other methods involved joint planning sessions of units of work with the aim being to utilise the expertise in the school or department in planning a particular subject emphasis. This school also tried to balance expertise when making appointments so that all members could participate in a coherent programme of staff development that was beneficial to the staff, the school and, by extension, the pupils.

Where there was a coherent policy existing within a school and individual targets were fed into a defined staff development structure, or where there was a mechanism for departments to feed their needs into the school development planning, then whole school INSET had been provided. Schools in both Cumbria and Northumberland organised courses, for staff and students, about bullying as this was a concern expressed during the appraisal cycle by a number of staff in these schools.

In all schools the advent of the National Curriculum and the needs of the Key Stages have led to considerable concern among teachers and highlighted the need for in-service training and staff development. In LEAs that organise their administration into first, middle and high schools this has been of particular concern due to the transfer ages of the pupils. In these areas there has been considerable staff development across the phases and in all the relevant feeder schools. One middle school in Northumberland organised a series of twilight sessions to draw up a common approach to subjects, particularly French, while a high school organised similar twilight sessions on Key Stage 3 English.

(b) Higher education institutions
A small but significant number of those interviewed had attended courses run by their local university. Courses in classroom management, personal management or management skills were found valuable in terms of people's own personal development. Two schools entered into a partnership with a local university to devise and deliver a school-based management course as a result of a need defined through the mechanism of appraisal. A few individuals had embarked on further study in terms of higher degrees with one school providing a half-day's unpaid leave to allow a teacher to pursue this higher qualification.

(c) LEA INSET
Two large comprehensive schools in this research were grant maintained so this category did not apply.

Others expressed concern that the LEAs were no longer able to offer the extensive range of support related to in-service training as had once been the case. Courses were seen as useful, but the popular ones were over subscribed and the less mainstream and more innovative courses often had to be cancelled through lack of support as a result of diminishing budgets.

(d) Other
Self-motivated support was one of the most common methods used to meet professional development needs. Schools within pyramids were brought together to compile common programmes to meet the demands of the National Curriculum, departments were brought together to identify and discuss realistic targets, individuals embarked on evaluation and further study.

A number of respondents were able to visit other schools or departments as a means of sharing good practice, having made contact with colleagues teaching in circumstances similar to their own.

Others expressed cynicism at the quality of training offered by 'agency provision'. These individuals had a far greater self-belief, and a feeling that 'in-house' training was not only of a higher standard but also made economic sense. One headteacher, having gone through the appraisal process three times in the school and knowing the strengths of all the staff, was delighted to be able to utilise the expertise within his school for the purpose of mutual support and staff development. Much depends on the quality of the external provider. A knowledgeable, skilled person can bring a breadth and depth of insight to a subject which is not available in the school. Before you employ someone, decide exactly what you want and ask for a guarantee of delivery.

9 What contribution do you think the appraisal process generally had made/will make to:

(a) School development planning
These questions were included in the research in order to ascertain whether the reservations expressed formerly, relating to the isolation of appraisal, still applied. We were also interested to see how far there was a development towards coherent policies of appraisal and staff development in schools today.

In raising the question in one LEA in the early research, the appraisal team was seeking to establish how far appraisal had already been assimilated into the life and work of schools using a holistic approach, which linked, or sought to link, relevant aspects of planning, management and pupil's learning. In schools where interviewees considered appraisal as a bolt-on activity or as simply an extra job to be done, or where lines of communication for development planning and appraisal were not made clear, then responses tended to be negative. This pattern of responses was repeated in all the later research.

Where teachers, whatever their position in the school, were involved in the school development planning process they were confident that appraisal did inform those processes related to staff development and curriculum planning. It is also significant that, in the schools where a positive response was forthcoming, there was an open approach to appraisal and a recognition of its significance in informing staff and whole school development planning. In one school the headteacher and the staff had jointly identified a whole school need for the development of differentiation in teaching and learning. A decision was reached that every teacher should adopt this aspect of teaching and learning as one of their focuses, adapting the more general title of differentiation to a more specific focus that fitted into their individual needs. This clear example of how the appraisal system can be used to link appraisal to school development planning, staff development and the quality of education for pupils stands as a beacon of direction for other schools to follow.

All too few answers to these questions in the later research demonstrated an awareness of this holistic approach. Some felt sure that appraisal should inform school development planning but were not sure that it did. Comments in one LEA ranged from 'To be honest I don't know, but it should do', 'It could do but I feel it tends to raise all sorts of demands that simply cannot be met in terms of resources' to a more positive belief that 'Many of the issues arising from appraisal have been catered for in INSET sessions on training days.' Others still view appraisal in isolation, feeling that the senior management teams draw up development plans without consulting the staff or referring to appraisal statements.

Many schools in Cumbria, for example, were very aware of the need for a holistic approach to school management and were working hard to put in place structures that will allow the many separate channels of communication to feed into school development planning. Most staff development officers demonstrated their frustration at the confidentiality of the statements, feeling that this was among one of the strongest deterrents in allowing these structures to function effectively.

Others saw the need for more school focuses to be fed into the system. Some saw the priorities identified from their OFSTED report as acceptable targets to be incorporated not only into school and departmental plans, but targets that could be fed into the appraisal mechanism. This was seen by several schools as an effective means of reinforcing their development priorities, a way of improving the quality of education for the pupils and of raising standards. In one school it was felt that current appraisal was too non-judgemental and the whole school, in consultation with all staff, needed to arrive at criteria on which to judge not only management skills but also teaching skills. A Cumbrian school has also evolved a system whereby one person in each department is responsible for staff development. This person, in turn, feeds departmental needs into management and curriculum planning. This has the outcome of effectively involving more people in the management process and will ultimately lead to more positive responses to the mechanism of appraisal.

A large comprehensive school in Newcastle has, through discussion and agreement, managed to break the deadlock on the confidential aspect relating to individual target setting which they felt to be a barrier to articulating a coherent development plan for the school. Now the targets in this school, from all those appraised (including all non-teaching staff) are given to both pastoral and departmental heads. It was felt by all involved that this mechanism would help to ensure a more coherent input into school development planning. The school has also arrived at an umbrella focus in their development planning, under the broad heading of 'maximising achievement'.

An initial training day was then organised where small cross-curricular groups discussed two main points:

1. In order to raise achievement we should…
2. If this happened the outcomes could be measured by…

These ideas have formed the basis of all the school's priorities and their targets for the following year and will now be modified by each individual in the school to form a focus in their appraisal cycle. This model provides an excellent example of how to link school development planning and appraisal to directly improving the quality of education for the pupils. It also neatly incorporates the ideas expressed by a school in another LEA of the need both to involve all staff in the process and to determine performance indicators to assist in monitoring the progress and effectiveness of the targets set.

(b) Improving the quality of education for pupils
Most people interviewed confirmed that, within the context of their individual classroom and particular teaching styles, they felt that the quality of education for pupils had improved. Some teachers

identified rather idiosyncratic improvements, often relating only to the material conditions of the classroom which they felt would benefit the pupils. Examples ranged from wishing for a new filing cabinet to more sockets in the language classroom. Others were more esoteric and generalised in their beliefs relating to improved standards. Respondents discussed such things as a more positive atmosphere or generally more awareness existed in the classroom, or that perspectives had been widened or morale improved, but were unable to be more specific. This perhaps points to the need to not only identify targets after the focus but also to define some performance indicators to accompany any targets that are being set.

Some teachers were able to be more specific, but again mostly on an individual level rather than within the context of a whole school perspective. These respondents referred to such improvements as: 'Thinking more carefully about task setting and appropriate teaching styles'; 'I am much better at planning, and the tasks I give to pupils are now more sharply focused'; 'I have improved the pace of my lessons'; 'I give clearer instructions'; 'I can cope with mixed ability teaching better'. These comments represent an amalgamation of some of the main areas discussed.

(c) More effective management
Where appraisal was seen to be replacing what had been effective existing systems of staff development, there was on occasion some negativity. However, only a few schools in our later studies referred to any earlier systems of staff development. This is possibly explained by the fact that appraisal is now seen as part of the structure of the school's monitoring system, if not an integral part, and that earlier models have now become history.

A surprising number of respondents simply admitted to not knowing whether appraisal had led to more effective management. Others, and not all of them by any means main scale teachers, fobbed off the responsibility of management, believing that it had nothing to do with them – that's what the headteacher and senior management team are paid to do. This demonstrates a sometimes familiar danger of lack of communication and isolationist management techniques.

In Northumberland answers were more tentatively positive, with teachers often feeling that the appraisal system, in theory, should have helped management but were still not quite sure how. 'I think the management are better informed to make management decisions' was one response. Others felt that it must make a difference as it identified concerns, needs and aspirations which must make development planning more effective. It was also felt to be providing communication channels which for many staff were not there previously. Another respondent pointed out that it was also providing opportunities for staff to see how others work and encouraging a team spirit. We seem to be moving nearer to the more effective spirit of a holistic management approach.

In our later research a considerable number of teachers expressed a strong belief that their job was to teach and that the rest was a 'management issue – not mine'. While most senior staff saw the need for a coherent policy of school development, and individual development planning leading to enhanced education for pupils, this did not seem to have filtered through to the majority of the staff.

OVERALL FINDINGS AND CONCLUSIONS

Where appraisal was found to be most effective there was invariably a background of sound relationships and trust. Indeed in many schools, especially the smaller primary and middle schools, appraisal was seen as a valuable tool for bringing the staff together and improving relationships.

In many cases appraisal focuses were seen as effective for individuals but lacking relevance in terms of whole school planning. There were, in all three main studies we undertook, excellent examples where an open style of management involved all teachers in school development planning so that all members of staff felt an ownership of policies and planning strategies and therefore welcomed the inclusion of school-initiated focuses for their appraisal. Since all departments are now required to produce development plans, where these were also used to inform school development planning (and vice versa) all staff became involved in the planning processes and, therefore, felt a greater ownership of the priorities identified.

Processes for prioritising needs, requiring the consultation and involvement of all staff, provide individuals, at all levels, with insight not only into their own professional developmental needs but also into the wider needs of department and school. This can then mean that individuals approach appraisal with shared insights. The school development plan and departmental development plan then can clearly indicate major thrusts of school policy for the future. Priorities are understood by all and can be used as a backdrop when considering areas of focus in the appraisal system.

To assist in the maximisation of the effects of appraisal, training should perhaps lay greater emphasis on self-appraisal and how to arrive at a focus, which is easier if the school has already determined an umbrella priority. This priority can then be tailored to an individual teacher's classroom needs. It is easy to feel inhibited in a choice of focus if left without guidance or rigorous, honest self-appraisal. Choice is often driven by what is observable rather than the focus leading to the observation. If there is a relevant focus that does not appear to lend itself to observation then the idea of data collection can be introduced for that focus, and a separate focus agreed to include observation. However, many areas that at first seem not to have an observable element do so on closer examination. For the many teachers who have expressed difficulty in deciding, surely a school-based focus would help.

In schools where appraisal is seen as effective, mechanisms exist for all targets requiring action to be fed into the school development planning processes. This can be done in a number of ways:

(1) by the INSET coordinator or staff development officer receiving targets;
(2) by pastoral and departmental heads having access to the targets and feeding them into the staff development structure;
(3) by the headteacher, who receives both the statement and the targets and who must have access to any school development plans.

Staff development programmes are more effective where an open, consultative approach to determining targets is chosen and where a coherent and holistic approach to the management of change is adopted. If schools have not yet devised a coherent, holistic structure for both school and staff development planning then at the very least themes of targets that emerge from appraisal should be recognised by senior management as pointers to action demanding some priority.

In many schools the formal structures required to link all the aspects of school management, including curriculum planning, appraisal and staff development, in a coherent and beneficial way have not yet been fully developed. Where initiatives are viewed as separate, appraisal is seen as a bolt-on burden. It is now especially urgent in this climate of more initiatives and pressure that the demands of the existing National Curriculum, OFSTED inspections and school development planning are not seen as merely separate, non-related burdens, but are integrated into whole school planning and management. The increasing role of the Teacher Training Agency in determining where funding for continuing professional development is allocated is perhaps the most telling sign of the need to examine these areas.

3

Arriving at a Focus for Appraisal

WHY HAVE A FOCUS?

Circular 12/91, paragraph 19 stated that: 'The appraiser is entitled to appraise performance across the full range of professional duties undertaken, including temporary responsibilities. Appraisal should be undertaken on the basis of an established job description.' The first sentence is an interesting one, giving rise to a series of thoughts which are explored in this chapter.

Paragraph 20 continued: 'Appraisal is more likely to be purposeful if it focuses on specific areas of a school teacher's work. This will be particularly so with the appraisal of headteachers, deputy heads and other teachers with a wide range of managerial duties.' The job of a teacher is far too large to be appraised in any one appraisal cycle and therefore focusing on different aspects of the job in different appraisal cycles is a more productive use of time. However, it can also be argued that a greater purpose may be served in appraising the whole job.

ONE FOCUS OR MORE?

This is entirely up to the appraisee and appraiser, as the two have to manage the process in the time allotted. The only real parameter is that the work focused on includes a classroom observation.

WHO CHOOSES THE FOCUS?

In successful appraisal the area or areas of focus are negotiated between the appraiser and appraisee, with the appraisee having the major share of the decision. In making this decision both participants should bear in mind school development plans and departmental and curriculum needs. This is not to say, however, that the appraiser has no say in the process, she or he *should* have a say.

HOW IS THE FOCUS CHOSEN?

One of the questions we are most often asked about appraisal is, 'How do I choose a focus?' This is related to a number of factors which we discuss below.

Matching appraisers and appraisees

Crucial to the success of appraisal is the matching of appraiser and appraisee. This in many cases becomes a clear determinant of what a focus will be, often for reasons of personality. There are cases where a teacher has chosen a particular focus because their appraiser has much to offer in a certain area and, therefore, they feel they can derive more benefit by choosing this area. There are times when a focus has been chosen as a safe option, for instance when someone has been working with an appraiser for whom they have little to no respect.

Other teachers have chosen certain areas of focus based on what they want to target at the end and in the belief that their appraiser has sufficient 'clout' in the hierarchy to provide this for them. As much of the thought goes into choosing a focus before the appraisee/appraiser match is made, and even more after it, how are matchings taking place? In some instances teachers are not aware of how the matchings are made, they simply happen. This is not seen as best practice and we suspect will lead to focuses being chosen on the safe option side.

Circular 12/91 said that wherever possible the appraiser should already have management responsibility for the appraisee and where this is not the case the headteacher should appoint a person who is in a position, by virtue of their experience and professional standing, to ensure the appraisal serves the needs of both the appraisee and the school. However, it is possible to interpret management responsibility flexibly.

So what does 'management responsibility for...' mean? This has been interpreted widely in schools throughout the country. As referred to earlier some schools have made a straight line management process their way of interpreting this. In those schools where maybe this was the expected way of operating this has been on the whole successful. In others it has caused problems, particularly where there has been a lack of respect from appraisees with regard to their managers. In these instances paragraph 22 of Circular 12/91 has been invoked. This stated that headteachers should not refuse requests from staff for an alternative appraiser if there are particular circumstances which suggest this might be appropriate. Despite the Circular stating that such circumstances are likely to be exceptional there has been a liberal definition of 'exceptional'.

Some schools have deferred to the second part of the statement for their matching, using either a cross-curricular approach or simply having an agreement on who the appraisee, appraiser and headteacher agree should be the appraiser. Providing agreement can be reached in this way, and the appraiser is seen to have the experience and professional expertise needed as an appraiser, this perhaps is the most effective method.

One popular misconception that has arisen is that appraisees may choose their appraisers. This is not true. The matching of the appraisee with appraiser is the responsibility of the headteacher. How headteachers choose to interpret this is their responsibility, but allowing appraisees to choose appraisers is a potential recipe for disaster. In some schools pairing has taken place but not always happily. Many teachers will have unhappy memories of their own school days – gloomily waiting till last to be included in the team!

We are often asked whether the matching of appraiser should be made after the appraisee has chosen their focus. In an ideal world this may well be the case. Appraisal is full of paradoxes and one of these concerns confidentiality. On the one hand teachers often tell us that they would like their appraiser to be matched on the basis of their focus but they do not feel it is right for the headteacher, or other person who has to make the matching, to know what their focus is. A further paradox is that the headteacher sees each statement and is therefore aware of the focus anyway. If the removal of this aspect of confidentiality can facilitate the matching being done after the focus, then we would recommend it.

Useful prompts to help select the focus

How do teachers actually arrive at focus areas? For some it is a simple process: teaching is their job and that is what they will focus on. For others it is more complex: teaching is their job but that in itself is too large and complicated to focus on so they choose an aspect of teaching that they feel comfortable with and wish to look at to see what they can learn from this area. Others see appraisal as an opportunity to spend dedicated time working in confidence with a trusted colleague, focusing on an area of their work that they do not feel happy with. Again the appraisee/appraiser relationship comes to the fore.

For some teachers however the process is more complex: should they focus on their teaching or on a non-teaching aspect of their work? Although Circular 12/91 indicated that focusing on a particular aspect of work may be more purposeful for those with a wide range of managerial duties, classroom observation remains compulsory for everyone except headteachers, whatever their focus.

Figure 3.1 shows a model used in a school we have worked with which they found useful. The prompt list below was used as a starting point for identifying suitable areas as a general focus on the first observation and may now serve as a starting point for negotiating an individual teaching analysis. School groups may choose to meet together and adapt this prompt list to meet their own needs, thus agreeing on a different starting point common to their school.

General Focus – Prompt List

The terms used below were identified as possible indicators of the aspects of teaching defined by each of the headings in capital letters.

1. TEACHING SKILLS
   - control
   - planning and preparation
   - organisation
   - communication
   - flexibility
   - review

2. LESSON CONTENT
   - knowledge of subject
   - choice of materials and resources
   - dealing with children of different abilities in the same group

3. TEACHER – PUPIL INTERACTION
   - relationships with pupils
   - use of language in the classroom
   - questioning techniques
   - awareness of differing individual needs and abilities

4. PUPIL LEARNING
   - children 'on task'
   - evidence of pupil interest and involvement
   - pupil written work
   - pupil verbal responses
   - pupil practical work
   - evaluation of pupil work

---

5. TEACHING METHODOLOGY
   - tasks selected
   - match with school guidelines
   - teaching style(s) adopted
   - motivation
   - reinforcement
   - recapitulation

6. LEARNING ENVIRONMENT
   - display work by children
   - teacher display work
   - relationship between materials available and session content
   - practical equipment available and used

7. PERSONAL QUALITIES
   - energy
   - enthusiasm
   - flair
   - flexibility
   - sense of humour

The above list is by no means exhaustive, neither will all statements be relevant to all circumstances – hence its suggested use is as a starting point for discussion.

Figure 3.1 *Model for prompt list*

The answer to the dilemma of 'what focus?' is to have two or more areas of focus. One of these must be a classroom-based focus, such as using an appropriate range of teaching skills, and can have classroom observation. The other, which may be managerial or non-teaching, does not have to have an observation component. Some teachers choose an area of focus which is basically management but has a bearing on their teaching and can be observed in the classroom.

Questions related to whether a teacher should focus on something they are good at or on an area of perceived weakness abound. This area of perception is one that is often not given real credence when teachers are considering what they should focus on. In some schools it is quite daunting to be prepared to focus on something that you feel weak at while in others it is already part of life through an existing review process.

For some teachers using the self-appraisal sheets included earlier has helped to firm up a focus, but for those wanting other ideas the following may be useful.

Management approach

A simple way to arrive at a focus is to answer the following questions:

- What is the key *purpose* of my job?
- What key *function* do I have to perform to meet this purpose?
- What do I have to be *competent* at to perform the function?

The focus is then on one or all of the competencies.

Matrix approach

The matrix approach (see Figure 3.2) to problem solving is not new, though treating this as a Bingo approach may be! The matrix can be used as a line across, a line down, or a full house, but corner to corner does not count in this game. If this does nothing else it may bring a little light relief to some of the tensions some teachers feel in focusing. There are of course no rules to say that the focus has to be decided by the teacher alone. Why not enlist the help of a colleague or partner in the process and get a different perspective to help with your deliberations?

To obtain a line across take one of the elements in the vertical column and complete the horizontal line against this by filling in whatever activities you engage in under this heading. You will finish up with one completed line and all the rest blank. It should then be

F \ R	Self	Pupils	Curriculum	Admin.	Staff	External
Planning and Preparing						
Teaching						
Communi-cating						
Managing						
Monitoring						

R = Responsibilities; F = Functions

Figure 3.2 *Example of matrix approach to choosing a focus*

easier to choose a specific focus from one of the boxes. The vertical line works in exactly the same way. The full house needs you to take time at the end of a day to fill in the tasks you have undertaken during the day in whichever box seems appropriate, sometimes more than one. At the end of a week some boxes will be overflowing and others nearly empty. Are they overflowing because you feel particularly good about this aspect of work and, therefore, spend a lot of time on it, or because conversely you really struggle with this aspect and, therefore, spend a lot of time on it? Either answer is a good reason to focus on what exactly it is you do in this area, what your strengths and weaknesses are and how this is evidenced through observation or data collection.

What about the boxes that are nearly empty? Again apply the same criteria, is it because you have real strengths in this area and therefore do not need a lot of time there, or because you have weaknesses and try to avoid these areas like the plague?

Matrix to metaphor

From the sublime to the ridiculous may be to use the simple idea of drawing a tree to help clarify a focus. As you can see from Figure 3.3 the core, or trunk, is teaching. The large branches are branches of teaching, the smaller ones are the subdivisions from the branches, the twigs and leaves still smaller subdivisions. A focus may emerge as the trunk, large branch, twig or leaf. This approach works well for some people when deciding on a focus with others rather than alone, and it can be good fun. One teacher said this was fine as long as you were undertaking appraisal in the spring or summer when there were plenty of branches and leaves, but what would happen in the autumn or winter? A quick-witted colleague replied that appraisal was evergreen!

FOCUS IN CONTEXT

Earlier in this chapter we mentioned that Circular 12/91 indicated that appraisal should serve the needs of both the teacher and the school. In order to do this areas of focus must be chosen where benefit may be seen to both. This in itself raises one of the most contentious areas of appraisal. Since its introduction the aims of appraisal, clearly stated in the Regulations, have at times been interpreted to mean that appraisal is only for the personal benefit of the appraisee and that target outcomes should only be to this end. This is clearly not an interpretation the government would put on appraisal, nor do we believe it is one most teachers put on it. The majority of teachers will

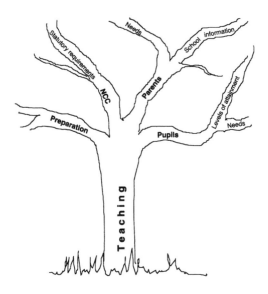

Figure 3.3 *Teaching 'tree' model, clarifying focus of appraisal*

see that the greatest benefits are to be derived from appraisal when at least one focus is linked to a priority item in the school or departmental development plan.

One LEA and a number of schools have taken this principle to heart by agreeing that at least one focus for every teacher will be the same as one emanating from the school development plan or, in the case of some secondary schools, departmental plans. At first sight this may appear to be a takeover of the appraisal process by the school and lead some teachers to feel that this was always going to happen, that they were sold appraisal as being beneficial to them as individuals but it is now being seen as of greater benefit to the school. We do not see it this way but as a strengthening of the position of the individual.

FOCUS AND SCHOOL DEVELOPMENT PLANS

Each teacher has a right and responsibility to be involved in the production of the school development plan, not just play a lip-service role. Different schools have different ways of doing this but what is important is that certain criteria are in place:

- Each teacher is aware of the vision and goals for the school as expressed in the development plan and in any mission statement that exists.

73

- Each teacher is well aware of how the school development plan priorities have been arrived at.
- Each teacher can see how her or his job leads towards achieving the vision.
- Each teacher knows that the school has a commitment to the ongoing development and training of all staff.
- Each teacher knows the mechanism through which their views related to the school development plan are taken into account and how progress towards achieving the plan is monitored, evaluated and fed back.

In this scenario appraisal plays a natural part in enabling teachers to see how they are contributing to the overall success of the school and what they need to further this and, at the same time, they know that the school has a publicly stated commitment to their development and training, thus leaving the way open for individual areas of focus and targets to be achieved.

If one focus is related to a priority area of the school development plan surely the reviewing that will take place within appraisal, with its subsequent target outcomes, will ensure that resources are well used to achieve that priority. Equally, if a teacher targets a further area of their work for appraisal they do so in the knowledge that any resulting target, even though it does not have a direct relationship to a school priority area, will stand more chance of being met. This has much to do with motivation. We are aware of many teachers who have produced targets from appraisal, the achievement of which has only an indirect bearing on their work, but which has a direct bearing on how they feel in their job.

Let us quote two examples of this. A primary school in the north of England has a policy of one target area being related to a school priority area, with an agreement that all possible resources will go towards meeting targets from this. However the school development plan also has a budget for individual, non-plan related appraisal targets. One member of staff recently targeted a Masters degree. The school could not afford to pay all the fees for this but did agree to pay a percentage. The headteacher's rationale for this was twofold. First, the school had a commitment to the ongoing, continuous professional development of all staff. Second, the fact that the teacher could begin the course and have school support led to a greater sense of worth and motivation in the classroom. This manifested itself in a more relaxed attitude, return to a sense of humour, and using information gained on the degree course in the classroom.

In a secondary school the target was a Mountain Leadership

Course. This teacher took no part in the school's outdoor education work and was not a member of the PE Department; indeed, it came as a surprise to the headteacher to know that the teacher had such an interest. A grant was made towards the course, again motivation increased, and a group of students subsequently visited an outdoor location. Benefits to both teacher and school resulted from using one school-based and one completely individual focus. There are many examples such as these, but others where appraisal does not have the chance to operate like this. The question is, if some schools can do it why can't others? All have the same type of budget allocation and the same ability to use appraisal in this way.

FOCUS ON COMPETENCY OR INCOMPETENCY?

As appraisal moves into the second or even third cycle the question of what to focus on becomes more clearly defined. For some teachers there is still work to be done on the original focus, for others action was long since achieved and a second focus has begun during an existing cycle. With a continuous drive towards school effectiveness there is undoubtedly a move towards looking at the competency level of teachers. This for some is still emotive. It raises questions of what is competency, who defines it, who judges it, what happens if we are not competent etc.

Our view is that whatever focus someone chooses for appraisal it is about competency; the basic question they are asking their appraiser to address with them is 'How competent am I at doing this aspect or these aspects of my job?' If this question is not being asked then we wonder whether those critics of appraisal who see it as being too soft are perhaps right. The real issue at stake here is a justifiable apprehension on the part of teachers that appraisal is being turned, through the back door, into an assessment model far removed from its original aims. We would argue that if some of the strategies we have detailed are in place then the control of appraisal rests where it was always intended to be, in the school with the individual teachers. If the profession can prove that it has achieved the aims then there should be no need for fear. The fear should come if appraisal has not achieved its aims.

In 1995 teachers started to use competencies as a base for their focus area and many of them have been involved in mentoring with newly qualified teachers, who are used to working and being assessed on their competencies and see it as natural. Some mentors have seen that there can be benefits in looking at a directly specified aspect of work, having it observed and receiving feedback on it. Indeed several teachers have found that doing this made appraisal a lot simpler the second time around.

If the principle of using competencies is acceptable to some teachers, then where do the competencies come from? The DfEE a few years ago published an extensive list of such competencies. The net effect of this was to confirm some teachers' views that the Department knew little of what actually went on in classrooms, while leading others to believe that they were going to be tightly assessed. The lists disappeared on to the back burner but did not become extinct. The more recently published lists of competencies for newly qualified teachers have more than a passing resemblance to the originals, though they are certainly presented in a far more realistic form.

Whether the Teacher Training Agency will attempt to extend the competencies to all teachers is not yet known. Some teachers, working on appraisal focuses that have a management base, already use a competency approach. Some teachers use their appraisal process as a way of assessing where they are in terms of their management competency, as verified by an outside body, and use the target outcomes to improve themselves, again potentially providing individual and school benefits.

Some schools have agreed levels of competency themselves, as part of moves towards national awards or simply as a local initiative, and these are providing appraisal focuses.

An example of an agreed level of competence from a school in our research is shown in Figure 3.4.

The whole debate about competency seems to centre, not around using it for appraisal but around who provides the base line and what happens afterwards. An increasing number of modern, successful industries are making use of competency approaches to appraisal. We would not suggest that we blindly follow their lead, but we do suggest we take note of what is happening.

Achievement and Effective Teaching and Learning

Achievement

The achievement of any pupil should be commensurate with her/his potential. Standards of achievement should be judged against national norms and against the capabilities and previous attainments of an individual.

Criteria for effective teaching and learning

1. *Variety and range of materials and approaches*
   - A broad range of materials is available to ensure access to the curriculum.
   - A variety of resources are available to fit individual needs.
   - Different pupils are working on different tasks.
   - Materials and approaches are targeted appropriately at individual pupils.
   - A range of appropriate learning activities is available and appropriately used, ie
     - structured reading and writing tasks;
     - investigational, open-ended work;
     - collaborative group work;
     - experiential learning;
     - problem solving;
     - information handling.

2. *Motivation and enthusiasm*
   - Pupils are fully involved in the task.
   - Pupils are participating fully in the activity.
   - Pupils are engaged in a learning experience.
   - Pupils are discussing task activity.
   - Pupils know what is expected of them and can explain the task.
   - There is evidence of teacher giving praise, instructive criticism, enthusiastic encouragement and developing positive and supportive tone.
   - Pupils confidence and self-esteem are high.

3. *Individual needs: differentiation*
   - Teacher has knowledge of pupils' ability and learning patterns and personality.
   - Learning outcomes are matched to the individual pupils' needs, ability, interest and aptitude.
   - Teacher is communicating with individuals and/or small groups.
   - Time allowed for pupils to complete a task varies according to individual differences.
   - Support and extension is systematically planned.

4. *Classroom management; learning environment; classroom organisation*
   - The physical layout of the room is appropriate for learning activity.
   - There is evidence of routines for the beginnings and endings of lessons.
   - Pupils know what behaviour is expected of them for a variety of learning activities.
   - Pupils work is displayed in a way which shows it is valued.
   - Other displays provide a stimulus for learning.
   - A working atmosphere is maintained through effective communication between teacher and pupils.
   - Inappropriate behaviour is responded to appropriately and consistently. There is consistent use of sanctions and rewards.
   - Teacher responds to unexpected or unplanned situations.

5. *Planning and preparation*
   - Selection of educational aims and objectives is made in terms of learning outcomes for a lesson/number of lessons.
   - Approaches and resources are prepared and provided to deliver these.
   - Progression for individual pupils is built into the tasks/activities.
   - There is evidence that the lesson/number of lessons is part of a structured course.
   - Teachers have a secure knowledge of their subject.

6. *Communication*
   - Teacher makes clear the structure and purpose of the learning experience.
   - The teacher is successful in engaging the pupils in the learning experience.
   - The teachers use a variety of ways of communicating:
     - informing;
     - describing;
     - explaining;
     - discussion;
     - questioning.
   - There are appropriate interventions in the learning experiences of the pupils.
   - Pupils discuss work they are undertaking – this is part of the learning process.
   - Pupils read accurately, expressively and with understanding, using a range of books and other texts for learning.
   - Pupils writing coherently, fluently and accurately, tackling a range of work and planning and redrafting where appropriate.
   - Pupils speak clearly and audibly in a wide range of circumstances – they narrate, explain, describe, hypothesise, analyse, assert, compare, question and deduce.
   - Pupils listen to others and respond appropriately to what they say.
   - Pupils develop presentation skills both in speaking and writing.

7. *Numeracy*
   Pupils should be able to cope with mathematical demands of everyday life. In particular they should:
   - handle number and measurement fluently;
   - use calculators accurately and appropriately;
   - apply spatial concepts;
   - make sense of information presented numerically and graphically;
   - handle statistical information in everyday contexts.

8. *Evaluation and reflection*
   - There is evidence of the teacher evaluating recent experience and using information to determine future practice.
   - Evidence is shown of evaluation of pupil work and progress being related to individual pupils.

9. *Pupil participation, involvement, responsibility*
   - Pupils are involved in determining and identifying their own learning outcomes.
   - Where appropriate, pupils are given opportunities to choose the task, resources required and the way in which they work.
   - Pupils can identify and carry out appropriate behaviour in a variety of learning activities.
   - Pupils can identify their strengths and weaknesses and know what they need to do to improve their achievement.
   - Pupils retain and apply their knowledge, skills and understanding.

10. *Assessment*
    - There is evidence of mechanisms for both formative and summative assessment.
    - Assessment is part of teaching and learning and is built into classroom experience.
    - Record keeping systems are in place.
    - Evidence is kept to support teacher assessment.
    - Assessment is used in the planning.
    - The school and departmental marking policy is applied and informs assessment.

Figure 3.4 *Example of an agreed level of competence*

WHAT SHOULD A FOCUS BE?

Our research would indicate that whatever aspect of work the focus covers it should have certain criteria.

Manageable

Appraisal can be a time-consuming process, sometimes more time consuming than necessary. Whatever focus is chosen it has to be managed by the appraisee and appraiser in terms of time, resources and energy. These things need to be taken account of by the appraisee in suggesting the focus, by the appraiser in considering the focus and finally by both together in agreeing it.

Observable

The Regulations require that every teacher is observed teaching on at least two occasions in the first year of the appraisal cycle by one appraiser. The Regulations make no mention of time in this; but Circular 12/91 stated that observation should be for a total of at least an hour spread over the two occasions. This is unequivocal, though often grossly misinterpreted. This means that however many focus areas are chosen at least one must be capable of having observation of teaching, with measurable outcomes, agreed by appraisee and appraiser. It does not mean that every focus has to have an observation.

Relevant

A focus should be relevant to the job the teacher is doing as well as relevant to the school development planning. We constantly hear that there is not enough time for appraisal, so surely there is not enough time to look at focus areas that are irrelevant to the job or the school.

Developmental

A much maligned word! Some people seem to be disappointed when appraisal is billed as a developmental process and then does not produce development for them. No process can produce development by itself, only the people involved can make the process developmental. What does it mean anyway? It means that a focus is agreed that the appraisee wishes to look at in terms of what their current position is, and then how they can develop in this area. In the continuous improvement philosophy this is always possible, but only if people are open to accepting the philosophy. If they are not it is hardly surprising that some appraisals have not been developmental. There is also, of course, a requirement on the school to embrace a philosophy of continuous improvement, if improvement is to happen for individuals. The two people working together can embrace the philosophy; but if they hit the brick wall of indifference when it comes to targets and taking action then who can blame them if they pack up and reduce appraisal to another time-wasting hoop. Schools on the continuous improvement road towards effectiveness will, by nature, already be working in a developmental way.

Interesting

A focus that is interesting is more motivating and is more likely to produce effective results. Enough said!

Challenging

There has been much discussion about appraisal being hard or soft and not having any teeth. Our answer to this is that teeth are for biting and there are enough people trying to bite teachers at the moment without them doing it to themselves. What appraisal should be though is challenging – to the appraisee and the appraiser. The crux of this is, of course, the focus. Because of this some people would argue that only areas of weakness should be focused on. We would disagree. Choosing an area of focus based on something that a teacher feels she or he is good at has as much value as a weakness – with certain provisos:

- What should actually be focused on is what makes the teacher successful in this area, what are the strengths, what are the strategies used, how these are recognised and celebrated.
- Consideration is given to other areas of the teacher's work to which these strengths and strategies can be applied.
- Once the strategies and strengths have been recognised they should be targeted for development for the continuing benefit of the appraisee and also for other colleagues in the school.

Overall, it is perhaps more challenging to make an appraisal focus work when it is related to a successful area rather than a weakness.

We also know from working with colleagues that those teachers who have received benefits from appraisal in the first cycle are more likely to have the confidence to choose an area of perceived weakness the second time around, often only to have their perceptions denied through appraisal evidence.

Negotiated and agreed

The focus should be initiated by the appraisee, suggested to the appraiser before the initial meeting and negotiated during that meeting. Once it has been negotiated then it should not be changed or amended without the joint agreement of the appraisee and appraiser. If trust is to exist between the two, this negotiation is crucial.

Enjoyable

Appraisal should be fun and enjoyable. It should be a celebration and have a refreshing frankness about it. Working through a focus should be enjoyable too but it will only be so if both people are clear about the steps above. Go on, indulge yourselves, enjoy your focus!

IN CONCLUSION

Here are some areas of focus chosen by teachers:

- the effective organisation of a working environment in the classroom appropriate to the abilities of the children;
- the appropriate use of teaching and learning styles;
- effective communication with parents to promote children's learning and development;
- effective communication with and management of non-teaching staff;
- lesson beginnings, middles and endings;
- the management of behaviour;
- the effective and appropriate use of differentiation;
- how effective am I as a team member?
- the effectiveness of the implementation of the National Curriculum;
- effective departmental management;
- effective budgeting;
- making effective use of school policies and schemes of work;
- how effectively my job progresses in line with school/ departmental objectives.

These are broad, general areas of focus. It is essential that any areas of focus must have outcomes that are measurable. It is suggested that before a focus is agreed relevant performance criteria for each teacher are agreed.

4

Appraisal and Staff Development

In April 1995 appraisal moved into a new critical phase which could determine whether it lives or dies in its developmental form. This phase was prompted by the fact that specific appraisal funding available from the government was withdrawn. This was not a phenomenon which suddenly appeared – the DfEE had made it clear from the introduction of Appraisal Regulations in 1991 that direct funding would cease after four years. Direct funding was replaced by appraisal being eligible expenditure under GEST Activity 1 for School Effectiveness at least for the 1995–6 year, though this has not been continued. By placing appraisal firmly under this heading there has been a reinforcement of the view of appraisal continuing as a review and development process rather than a performance, pay related process. Also interesting in this respect is the fact that many commercial and industrial organisations are moving firmly towards a review and developmental approach to appraisal, linked in some cases to a competency based approach.

Nevertheless, the financial situation has left a vacuum for many LEAs and schools as they ponder on how to continue appraisal, particularly at a time when many teachers are coming to the end of the first or second appraisal cycle and are reflecting on their experiences of the process. Cuts in education funding have meant some schools indicating that they will not continue with appraisal until more funding is made available, particularly for the mandatory observation part of the cycle. As a result of these factors and the findings of our evaluatory work it is clear that if appraisal is to have a meaningful shelf life beyond its first cycle some things need to change in some schools.

1. Appraisal must be a key part of any school effectiveness

    programme for both individuals, teams or groups and the whole school.

2. There needs to be a consideration of how appraisal, or review and development, can be offered to all members of staff in a school, not just the teaching staff, as is already happening in some schools.
3. Appraisal can be a linking mechanism for such seemingly incompatible initiatives as OFSTED Inspections and the Investors in People Standard.
4. Appraisal must be more integrated into school development planning and must be a key player in any whole school staff development policy.
5. Targets or outcomes must be considered at an earlier stage than at the end of the interview. Realistic performance indicators must be devised to monitor success in the achievement of those targets.
6. High quality, accurately targeted professional development, within the school's resources of time, money and personnel, must use appraisal as a key identification mechanism.

This chapter will explore each of these issues and consider how appraisal can offer a coherence to unite them all as a key link in the chain towards whole school improvement. Where appraisal has become an internalised part of school management and staff development, it is a more rewarding process at an individual, team or group level and for the school as a whole. To survive, appraisal must be recognised by teachers as a mechanism through which high quality and accurately targeted professional development can be delivered, where individual and school needs are recognised and reconciled to available resources. The proof of this must be in the delivery of the aims of appraisal. The Teacher Training Agency, among others, is keen to see a positive move away from INSET provision to continuous professional development – continuous learning rather than small chunks of learning. A report from the Teacher Training Agency to the Secretary of State in the Autumn of 1996 will clarify this thinking.

    Let us consider each of the possible changes in turn.

1. Appraisal – a key part of any school effectiveness programme

The arguments over what constitutes an improving school continue to resound in educational debate. So, what is school improvement? The International School Improvement Project (ISIP) has defined school improvement as: 'A systematic sustained effort aimed at change in learning conditions and other related internal conditions in one or more schools, with the ultimate aim of accomplishing educational goals more effectively' (van Velzen *et al.* 1985).

As all schools seem to be striving towards this improvement we may ask what factors combine to produce an effective school. The answer is that no simple combination of factors can produce an effective school. However, much recent research has provided common key factors in effectiveness. Though not exhaustive, the list does give an indication of some of the common factors associated with effective schools thus giving an overview of what the effective school may look like. What the factors cannot do is to say *how* the school became effective. It would not be unreasonable to argue that as a school improves, it demonstrates a growing number of the characteristics of effectiveness.

By definition, a school which is improving and becoming more effective, is involved in significant change both at individual, team and whole school level. Every teacher in every school will be only too well aware of the effects of change over the past few years, and willing to admit that many of the changes have benefited education and given it a shake that it deserved. They will argue that some changes have been detrimental to sound educational improvement, providing diversions into side roads at a time when sticking to the motorway was hard enough. Some may well put appraisal in this category of diversion.

A number of consistent factors have emerged from research into school effectiveness, and it can be seen that a well-structured appraisal process could be a highly effective way of determining where individuals, teams and the school are on the journey through school improvement to school effectiveness. The headings below are an amalgamation of those identified in a significant number of recent publications, all of which are included in the Bibliography.

Participatory/professional leadership
Any of the areas under the school improvement or school effectiveness columns could provide a realistic focus for the appraisal of anyone in a leadership role in the school. Each area provides a direct basis for information to be gathered from other colleagues, making positive use of the data collection part of the appraisal process. Anyone carrying out appraisal using these aspects of their job for a focus could benefit from a meaningful review of their current position and determine the development and training needed to further them on their personal journey through improvement to effectiveness.

Shared vision and goals
Those schools where there is a shared vision and clear goals show a unity of purpose and demonstrate consistent practice, and this consistency extends to the appraisal process. Where teachers are able to see a vision of their school or department they want to see a route to their being part of the vision. Where a process of school review has been adapted before appraisal took place this has helped teachers focus more clearly on school priorities in making their own focuses. The model has since been used by a number of schools with teaching and non-teaching staff. The school improvement process looks at an evolutionary planning process, and surely this is what appraisal ought to be. Having worked through the first cycle of appraisal and learned from it, the process ought now to become a natural part of the planning process for individuals, departments and other groups. If we are supportive of a developmental model of appraisal, the development must be evolutionary rather than revolutionary.

Teamwork
Any study of effective organisations identifies teamwork as one of the major contributory factors for success. This teamwork must be alive and dynamic, not just another glib mission statement fading on the entrance notice board to the school. Effective teamwork is about shared aims and visions, about involvement, responsibility and accountability. The appraisal process provides a clear, confidential mechanism through which each individual can examine their own past present and future team role.

A learning environment
Much is said about schools being a learning environment for all. We have never thought of schools as being anything other than this, but there are some schools where the learning environment is centred almost totally on the children. It ought to be the right of every teacher to share in that enriching learning experience as part of their own continuing effectiveness. If this is so, and risk taking is seen to be part of the process, then staff need to be able to take the risk in a positive, secure environment. What do we provide for the children? A positive, secure environment in which we encourage them to take risks. How do we help children grow through this process? We, as teachers, provide them with mechanisms through which they can look at their present situations and feelings about an aspect of their work, learn from their previous efforts and explore the future. We offer them review sessions, we record successes in Records of Achievement. Appraisal can mirror the process for teachers.

Emphasis on teaching and learning
Our own evaluatory work on appraisal for this book, combined with discussions with many teachers, indicates that appraisal can be more closely linked to the teaching and learning process. For many teachers one of the effects of the changes in the 1980s and early 1990s has been to undermine their confidence in their work and methods. Teachers have an awareness and a willingness to practise a varied and appropriate repertoire of methods, learning and using new strategies. They can only do this in an atmosphere of support, where there is a clarity of purpose in the department or school. At its heart, through observation, appraisal provides the opportunity for two colleagues to work closely together to analyse, celebrate and build on new and existing strategies. Feedback is provided based not on opinion but on observed evidence. Those teachers tempted in the first round of appraisal to put on a 'show' lesson soon learned the futility and dissatisfaction of the exercise. It could be argued that teaching observation ought, in reality, to become teaching analysis.

Explicit high expectations
Appraisal ought to provide the opportunity for individual teachers to consider where they stand in terms of expectations. The effective school, and department where appropriate, will also have communicated what its expectations are, thus allowing each teacher to consider her or his position within it. Appraisal should then be a way of matching individual and school expectations and, through target setting and prioritising, finding ways of meeting such expectations for both the individual and the school.

Positive reinforcement
Appraisal is a prime mechanism available for all teachers to celebrate their successes, receive and give accurate feedback and reinforce ways of working. If this is not the case we would argue that the appraisal process is not operating effectively in the school.

Monitoring and progress
For all teachers, developmental appraisal ought to be about setting, monitoring and evaluating success and laying down further criteria for this to continue. It is being argued that appraisal should be related to teaching and learning and the techniques used in the classroom. The fact that classroom observation is a mandatory part of the appraisal process would seem to provide opportunity for using a monitoring and enquiry approach to appraisal. If observation grew into analysis, the process might become more meaningful.

Learning for all
As part of the move towards school effectiveness through school improvement INSET is working towards continuous professional development. If this is to happen there needs to be a process continuously to identify, monitor and review teachers' progress through their professional development. Appraisal, of course, provides the opportunity for this, through the appraiser and appraisee developing a critical-friend relationship, moving into coaching and mentoring and using appraisal as a feedback mechanism. Much of the success of this depends on the relationship between appraiser and appraisee, a theme explored in Chapter 5.

Home/school partnership
One of the characteristics of effective schools is that they recognise education and learning as a partnership of all involved in the school. Appraisal can have its role to play in this, either by teachers using partnership as a focus or targets being set around the growth of partnerships.

2. Offering appraisal to all members of staff

The Investors in People Standard is of growing attraction to schools and one of its requirements is that a process exists for regularly reviewing the training and development needs of all employees (Investors in People Standard 2.3).

Despite the growing interest from schools in IIP there has also been dissatisfaction expressed with appraisal. There may be a number of paradoxes here. First, appraisal is not required by IIP, only the fact that a process is in place for reviewing the training and development needs of people, and yet appraisal can be the mechanism through which the Standard is met. Some schools have established a separate review process for IIP while keeping appraisal for other purposes. This does seem to make an unreasonable demand on people's time and to be a duplication of effort. One of the difficulties in schools is reconciling the confidentiality of the appraisal process with reviewing training and development needs. Confidentiality needs to be clarified in schools. How can an adequate staff development programme be organised, using appraisal as an identification means, when the organiser does not have access to the information? We believe that while appraisal discussions should be confidential to appraisee and appraiser, targets need to be shared with those who need to know, in order that they may act.

A second paradox is that appraisal in its current form only exists for teachers, while IIP requires a review process for all staff. It would seem logical to use the appraisal process for the teaching staff while establishing the same opportunity for support staff. It can be argued that classroom observation cannot be provided for support staff. True, but task observation can, as can third-party data collection. If there is to be a move towards the school becoming a whole learning community then involving all staff in a review process is logical. A process already exists for teachers and its extension to all staff would be the next step. In our experience greater motivation is provided for both teachers and support staff when they are working on the same structure.

3. Appraisal – a linking mechanism

The Investors in People Standard has already been discussed as one of the moves towards school improvement and as a way of recognising standards set in the school. OFSTED, of course, is a part of the life of every school at the present time, either in preparing for it, being inspected by it, or in implementing the action plan arising from it. We have already briefly considered the role of IIP, but what of OFSTED? What do the inspectors demand of appraisal? Basically, the OFSTED Framework requires that an assessment is made of 'the effectiveness of the arrangements for appraisal and their effects on professional development'. This statement matches in essence the regular review of training and development needs required by IIP.

In the same OFSTED Framework paragraph there is a requirement that 'the efficiency and effectiveness of arrangements to extend the knowledge and skills of teachers and other staff' is inspected. Appraisal does provide a mechanism through which the extension of knowledge and skills can be identified, monitored and evaluated for teaching staff. There are a number of other requirements of OFSTED that the effective and efficient implementation of appraisal will help to fulfil. However, there is a noticeable trend in inspection reports to indicate that in some schools advantage is not being taken of the appraisal process in fulfilling such requirements.

4. Appraisal must be integrated into school development planning

Increasingly schools have a staff development process to link these elements. Typically this has three stages:
- the staff development policy, containing the aims of staff development in the school and staff entitlement;
- the staff development plan, which specifies detailed objectives and learning outcomes;

- the staff development programme, which contains all the staff development activities which will take place in line with the policy and plan.

The policy contains the principles on which staff development in the school is based and this would normally contain a statement that the prime needs identification comes from three sources: school development plan, departmental, team or year group plans, and appraisal. Within the agreed parameters of the policy, the plan and programme are drawn up by a staff development group and are given equal weight for consideration with other aspects which make up the school development plan, such as curriculum needs. In this way all staff recognise that they have equality of opportunity in the allocation of resources and that the best use is made of what is available. They also tend to realise that it is up to each individual to make greatest use of the appraisal process. For the process to work effectively there is a need for the staff development group to be aware of agreed appraisal targets, but only those requiring resources. The confidentiality of the discussions leading to targets is, therefore, never breached.

We believe appraisal also ought to be linked with the policy, plan and programme for staff development. In those schools where school development plans are written through *active* staff participation, teachers do have an understanding of school priorities and feel a collective responsibility for them. It is a logical step for teachers to consider how their own job affects, and is affected by, current school priorities and how they can influence future ones. The appraisal process is seen in such schools as a tool to be used both as a review and a needs identification mechanism. The argument for this is that appraisal provides a common thread from review to action, therefore appraisal has the potential for making the best use of increasingly scarce resources.

If the school development plan is seen as the backdrop for appraisal, the process becomes less a sideshow and more a main stage event, linking individuals and the organisations. The basis for this assertion is paragraph 11 of Circular 12/91 which stated:

> Appraisal should be set in the context of the objectives of the school, which will generally be expressed in a school development plan. Appraisal should support development planning and vice versa. The school's objectives in a particular year should be linked with appraisal, so that, for example, professional development targets arising from appraisal may be related to agreed targets and tasks in the development plan. Similarly appraisal targets, when taken together, should provide an important agenda for action for the school as a whole. Targets set during

appraisal should therefore meet the needs of the school as well as those of individual appraisees. Setting appraisal within the framework of school development should also ensure that targets are realistic and make the best use of available resources.

Newton and Mack (1994) see appraisal as 'important to the agenda', as valuable fuel for driving staff development programmes. Appraisal acts as one of the key methods of identification of needs, and the school development plan is seen as the backdrop for appraisal. In their article they discuss their school's staff development policy, which has three main aims:

- to provide continuing professional development for staff, teaching and non-teaching, permanent and temporary, supply staff and student teachers, including initial teacher training activity;
- to encourage individual members of staff to plan their careers and to identify and exploit career opportunities;
- to develop the staff's awareness of the school's philosophy, management plan, aims and objectives, and to enable them to contribute to their formulation and delivery.

This policy statement seems to encapsulate all the philosophical underpinning that we have been urging throughout this book. You might be thinking that this is all very ideological and not at all practical. But if these basic ideological premises are not considered together, then all training needs will be fragmented and will serve neither the individual nor the school. In these days of diminishing budget resources and increasing demands on time there is an even more urgent need to make the most out of development budgets. There must be some interconnection between the needs of the individual and the needs of the school, arrived at by an outline of clear school aims and objectives and supported by sound ideological precepts.

Newton and Mack go on to suggest that, with this policy clearly in place, 'implementation of the policy' becomes 'the corporate responsibility of all staff in a position to help with the professional development' aspirations of colleagues. This corporate responsibility is a crucial element and is fuelled by a very practical staff development practice, which again is in three stages:

- identification of needs;
- delivery of training;
- evaluation/feedback.

It would be useful to elaborate a little on each of these stages, as they all interlock, forming a continuous programme of development for both the school and the individual, thus improving standards for the ultimate benefit of the pupils. These stages also serve to reinforce the philosophical premises on which they are based. In other words the school has a practical, workable, structured system of putting policy into practice.

Identification of needs

This first stage, is where appraisal fits into their programme, especially for the personal development of staff. Where target setting involves INSET or related activity these are notified to the staff development coordinator and fed into the wider programmes. Appraisal can also be used as a mechanism to ascertain any trends within departments or whole school issues that have escaped notice from other channels of communication. A key element within this identification stage is that the school, with the help and consultation of its staff, then draws up an annual staff development and INSET plan, within the context of the school development plan.

As well as the system of appraisal to channel developmental ideas into INSET, the school has devised a training needs questionnaire, the responses of which are also collated. This questionnaire, coupled with information from appraisal, provides an additional source of information about subjects on which members of staff would be prepared to lead training, a doubly valuable asset. In-house training has a value in terms of the school being able to provide its own training and thus save money, and a value in terms of the individual by providing an opportunity for those leading the training to develop their own potential, itself a developmental activity.

Delivery of training

The second stage of the school's staff development practice is the delivery of the programme, which incorporates a wide range of activity. They argue that 'alongside participation and consultation' (in themselves a form of staff development) opportunities exist for such things as 'job rotation, delegation, temporary responsibilities/ promotions, work shadowing and industry placements'. Their training programme is both imaginative and flexible and uses the full range of resources available both in-house and beyond the school. They have created a set of complementary training programmes delivered in a variety of ways ranging from workshops and seminars to school visits, classroom observation, teacher research and INSET days. This successful training is always in the context of the perceived school needs and the underlying aims and objectives of their school: 'It pursues an aspect of staff development in a logical sequence, both for the school and for the individual; it results from very careful planning and involvement of staff before the event.' This involvement of staff in determining the content and structure of their development is the key to the success of any programme of training.

Evaluation and feedback
The third aspect of this school's system is that of evaluation and feedback. The giving and receiving of feedback is essential in both the microcosm of individual teacher appraisal and the macrocosm of school development planning. In Newton and Mack's school, evaluation is an integral part of the staff development process because those involved need to know how far each initiative has served the purpose for which it was designed. When making these assessments the school uses a wide range of evaluation strategies, ranging from informal conversations to the more structured discussion, and including brief written feedback using a questionnaire tailored to the aims and objectives of any INSET day.

One of the key aspects of the Mandeville School development strategy is the involvement of all staff in devising the programmes of developmental activities. Whether this be via the needs identified through their appraisal system, the objectives suggested from their questionnaires or the aims outlined in their school policy, it would appear that all members of staff are both informed and involved.

This involvement in devising programmes of staff development and training which appear to lead to greater motivation and effectiveness of any initiative is argued strongly by Kenneth Washington (1993). Washington carried out research in selected schools in the USA and Canada, and his findings appear relevant to schools in Britain. His questions and research related to the teacher's role in the staff development process, adding to the body of research that suggests that 'active teacher involvement increases the likelihood of success and tends to lead to a positive attitude toward the desired change'. His interviewees seemed to feel that teachers know best what their needs are and that their direct involvement makes any programme more meaningful. He also believed, from his research, that there was a higher personal satisfaction, improved morale, better interaction between staff and more emphasis on personal development. Teacher initiated programmes appear to heighten motivation and engender a sense that teachers can make a difference. In his summary of findings it was suggested that 'both teachers and principals feel that teachers should be actively involved in initiating, planning and implementing staff development programmes.' He argued that 'when teachers take responsibility for curriculum and instruction decisions they are more likely to identify areas that need improvement and commit themselves to making the necessary changes.' His conclusions endorse the philosophical standpoint we are suggesting:

> As we move towards the twenty first century a new definition in staff development is emerging. It is a definition that ascribes a major role to teachers and makes no distinction between personal and organisational development. Indeed joining the two and allowing teachers to develop programmes that benefit both the individuals and the organisation is perhaps the best way to achieve systematic change. In sum, the involvement of teachers in the staff development process requires a new way of thinking and interacting and most importantly is a step in the direction of teacher empowerment.

Appraisal can be an integral part of this process, not only as a way of empowering teachers but as a means of informing any school development programme and of utilising the strengths of all the staff, not only for their individual development but for the development of the school and for the benefit of the pupils.

5. Targets or outcomes must be considered early

In some schools teachers are left wondering whatever happened to their targets. This should not, and need not be the case. If targets are considered early enough in the appraisal, ie at the beginning, then the majority should be achievable. In the last resort the very least a teacher can expect from appraisal is to be told the reason why targets cannot be met. This is preferable to not knowing anything, though it is far from being satisfactory.

It is unfortunate that targets have all too often been seen as something set at the appraisal interview and not considered before. If this is the case it is hardly surprising that some are not met. Appraisal is about teachers looking at their current situation with an experienced, trusted colleague, and discussing feelings about an aspect or aspects of the job. This involves looking back at past experiences, as well as looking forward to future opportunities. The view needs a school-wide context, hopefully using the school development plan as a guide. Self-appraisal is where target setting should begin, and it should involve looking towards a situation in the future, ie outlining targets of current knowledge. This outline should be sketched in as appraisal progresses until a final picture is reached. We are not suggesting that targets are actually set before the interview. What we are suggesting is that the appraisee has a feel for what target may be within the realities of day-to-day activities in school.

The issue of confidentiality has dogged appraisal from the beginning, and still does so. We would always defend the confidentiality of individual appraisal discussions but we feel it is imperative that target outcomes are available to those who are able to take action to make them happen. Circular 12/91 stated that 'targets, when taken together, should provide an important agenda for action for the school as a whole. How 'when taken together' is interpreted may differ from school to school, but targets must be taken together and must provide an important agenda for action if the best and most equable use is to be made of resources. If targets are used in this way it also removes the potential for teachers to argue that their chances of having targets met increase in proportion to the seniority of the appraiser.

Appraisal targets should be a key mechanism by which staff needs are identified. These needs should also be considered as one of the main sources of information when the school development plan is being written. If they are not, a golden opportunity to make appraisal and school development planning a meaningful processes is lost.

There are ways in which this can happen. In some schools targets requiring resources or action from those beyond appraisers are given to the staff or INSET development coordinator, with the confidentiality respected. However, there is a minimum of information which the coordinator needs to work effectively. Similarly targets are often presented to governors in a non-attributable, aggregated form in order that they can take action, with only the chair of governors having a right of access upon request to teacher targets. Often it is the case that targets do not reach governors, but those targets which governors can implement should be made known to them. If they are not, there is less chance of the targets being met. For example, governors may know the school's toilets need some refurbishment but may be unaware that all members of the French department have targeted new language facilities.

When targets have been agreed then two simple questions, related to identifying performance indicators, need to be asked:

1. What should I do in order to achieve this target?
2. If this happens, how can outcomes be measured?

6. Appraisal as a key identification mechanism

In moving forward to a more integrated developmental approach to appraisal, and with ever-increasing demands on the budgets in schools, there is an even more urgent need to find cost-effective ways of delivering staff development that is beneficial to both the school and the individual. Having used the appraisal process as a means of identifying the strengths and individual developmental needs of all the staff it is possible then to marry these individual needs, utilising in-house expertise, with the agreed developmental needs of the school.

A number of strategies can be adopted that will enable the school to use all these internal human resources in an efficient and cost-effective way. These allow schools to meet the full range of needs from the individual to the global, using the strengths that have been identified during appraisal, for the benefit of all. Here are a few suggestions that have been tried successfully in schools.

Staff Development Strategies
Shadowing   This is when a teacher has expressed an interest in gaining knowledge and expertise in another area within the school and attaches him- or herself to someone with that knowledge. Learning takes place 'on the job', in a similar way to the traditional trade apprenticeships. This strategy can be used in a variety of situations, for example with newly qualified teachers who wish to gain experience of pastoral duties. If such a teacher is attached, for the first year, or term, to another member of staff who is responsible for form tutor duties then the new teacher can gain experience and confidence while in a 'spectator role'. Gradually, as the new member of staff becomes more efficient, they can take over the responsibilities themselves. This strategy also applies to experienced staff who wish to expand their expertise by learning new skills in either teaching or management. If a member of staff wishes to gain knowledge and experience in the art of timetabling then that individual will attach themselves to the existing timetabler, again in a 'spectator role'. This strategy not only helps the individual in their staff development and enables them to apply for senior management positions but it also helps the school, which has another person with extra skills to whom it can delegate some responsibility.

Job sharing   This is a similar strategy to job shadowing, perhaps with wider implications. It is often used as a strategy in smaller primary schools where there is considerable team teaching and team planning. This method of staff development provides the opportunity for a teacher to gain confidence in a supportive environment and to expand expertise before trying things alone. It allows teachers to share experience. This is an equally effective strategy for extending classroom practice as well as for gaining pastoral and management experience .

Observation and analysis This is an extension of the other two strategies and is a very useful one to adopt if there is a particular skill that a member of staff wishes to acquire, or if a member of staff wishes to extend their repertoire of styles of teaching. A particular member of staff may lack confidence in developing group work or wish to observe some different teaching styles. This method of staff development provides an excellent opportunity to use existing expertise and allow teachers to observe a range of lessons. It has the dual function of making the giver feel valued and the receiver feel confident. It has obvious benefits in extending the teacher's range of skills and thus the pupils' range of learning experiences.

Bidding for initiatives Some schools keep a small reserve budget that enables them to offer allowances for a short time with particular initiatives in mind. This will vary according to the needs of the school, but could include a short-term allowance to review such things as equal opportunities. Alternatively, a school may offer an allowance for a term to review the effectiveness of appraisal, where the school has completed the first cycle, reached an 'implementation dip' of despondency and wishes to modify the arrangements for a more effective second round. Some teachers are willing to accept responsibility for short-term initiatives, without remuneration, either to develop their skills or simply as a challenge to their ability. Examples, in our research ranged from devising and implementing an assessment policy in the school to leading teams to explore curriculum innovation.

Short-term contracts This is also related to internal staff development, and is when an allowance is given for specific responsibilities for a specific period of time. Perhaps a person is given responsibility as second in department on a short-term basis or responsibility for exam entry on a fixed term. This can be used as a staff development strategy to give a person experience either of management within a department, or to give a person wider whole school management perspectives for a limited period of time.

Mentoring and buddy roles Another aspect of individual staff development is to offer a teacher the experience of mentoring. It is a valuable experience to feel able to act as a professional friend to a newly qualified teacher. It raises the self-esteem of the mentor and provides invaluable support for a new teacher. This strategy serves as an efficient and productive form of professional coaching for both the new teacher and the mentor. The mentor, or buddy, is usually an extra support, as part of a wider induction programme.

Rotating responsibility   This could include such things as rotating responsibility for library provision, the school magazine or the more simple tasks of taking minutes at a meeting, presenting topics at meetings or rotating the chair. This is an excellent and painless way to extend and encourage a considerable number of people's developmental potential. It is an easy method of staff development to swap responsibilities, either in the short or long term, if the outcomes are seen to be beneficial to all concerned. When rotating responsibilities it is essential the those wishing for promotional opportunities to senior management positions are given opportunities to develop their presentational skills.

Assembly   Rotating responsibility for assembly provides just such an opportunity. Presenting assemblies is an excellent experience for all. Most teachers, while confident in their classroom, feel threatened in front of a larger audience, especially one that consists of their peers as well as the students. What better way to gain confidence than to be involved. This strategy will elicit a sigh of relief from other members of staff as the burden is shared. It also reduces the all-too-easy criticism, as others know it will soon be their turn.

Providing time or supply cover   This can be the offering of protected non-teaching time in return for completing some departmental initiative, whole school project or creative curriculum innovation. If the timetable does not allow non-teaching time this strategy assumes that supply can be bought in, for an agreed time each week, until the project is finished.

Sabbatical or teacher placements   Few schools can afford this luxury but there are organisations and colleges willing to offer places for teachers for a term of study on a particular subject if the school will release them. This could be arranged during the quieter summer term when the pressure of examinations is over, at least in some secondary schools. A more affordable alternative is making use of teacher placements. Many thousands of teachers have already benefited from this initiative, enabling teachers to spend periods of time, from a day to a year, in a different environment, educational or industrial. This is a form of development opportunity which offers excitement and a really different learning opportunity. Each Training and Enterprise Council is able to offer advice on teacher placements in its area.

Coopting   This was a strategy used in one school not only as a means of staff development, but also as a means of raising self-esteem. Heads of department, pastoral and year heads had the opportunity to be coopted for one year on to the senior management team, with many benefits for the individual and the school. The senior management team benefited by having a new and different perspective, which gave a new input into their decision making process. The individual benefited by being given a wider perspective on management issues when they might have previously considered topics only from a partial perspective.

Involvement in INSET   When a whole school need has been identified then it is quite possible that the expertise is available within the school. When a programme of staff development activities is being devised and budgeted it is possible that existing members of staff, on a voluntary basis, will agree either to input sections of a whole day's programme or to offer short twilight sessions to share their expertise with other members of staff. This can be effective where a school decides to devote a training day to assessment or differentiation, for example, and a variety of staff lead different sections in the day's programme. It can also work with a more varied programme of activities, where some members of staff offer input on a variety of topics and the rest of the staff opt for the sessions that meet their particular needs or interests.

Joint school venture   It is possible that a neighbouring school has expertise in introducing an initiative which it is willing to share with you, or vice versa. Either way, joint school ventures are good staff development for all concerned. Those who give develop their presentational skills, not to mention their self-esteem and confidence. Is there anything more flattering than being regarded as an expert? Those who receive benefit in a broadening of knowledge and expertise.

Visiting other schools   If a neighbouring school has some expertise that you wish to take advantage of but they cannot spare the time for input on a training day, a good alternative is for a single member of staff to visit that school and then cascade the knowledge, either within their department or the whole school.

Piloting LEA initiatives   For those involved piloting provides a useful extension to their skills and development. It provides valuable resources, both human and economic, for the school, as well as increasing the status and reputation within the LEA and in the wider market place of the catchment area.

Work experience   Many LEAs offer this facility to teachers. Work experience can offer valuable insight to teachers on other options open to them and broaden their horizons. The placement can also be related to a particular curriculum area or administrative task. The examples are wide and varied and range from placements in food factories for production and marketing skills related to food science to placements with art and theatre groups related to the introduction of theatre studies or drama and placements in companies that have experienced successful promotional strategies. This is especially apt at present when there is an increasing need to market schools as a commodity as well as a service. This process is similar to teacher placements but is often arranged on a more local basis.

Exchange   In some schools there exists the possibility for teachers of equal status to experience a similar role in a different school for an agreed period of time.

We hope that the ideas above have indicated the wide range of possibilities available to schools in widening INSET into continuing professional development.

5

Training for Appraisal in the Future

For those teachers who are now entering the profession, appraisal should become a part of their working lives. However the need for training which has underpinned the introduction of appraisal should not go away, it should change its nature. We believe that there will be a need for training, or other forms of development, for the following teachers:

- newly qualified teachers;
- those being promoted to a post which is significantly different from their current post, including deputy heads and headteachers;
- those moving schools or LEAs;
- those returning to teaching after a lengthy period of absence.

We would also suggest that there should be the opportunity for appraisees to work together on a skills review basis, maybe at the end of a two-year cycle, to ensure that appraisal meets current needs. Each of these groups will have their own training needs, and we will try to address what we see them as being and how they can be met. Later in the chapter we will discuss the types of skills, which it may be useful to work on, for ongoing training.

NEWLY QUALIFIED TEACHERS

As the status of newly qualified teachers has altered more than any other for appraisal, we have included an extended section on their role in Chapter 6.

TEACHERS PROMOTED TO NEW POSTS AND MOVING TO OTHER SCHOOLS

For those being promoted to a substantively different post in a school, training needs may be a matter of spending time with their appraiser, reviewing how a focus may change and how this will be dealt with. This will be the case if the change takes place part-way through an appraisal cycle, which of course is likely. It is in situations such as this that the skills of the appraiser in questioning may need sharpening and appraisers have benefited from specific skills training, sometimes provided from within a school and sometimes by an outside provider. The essential differences between a current post and a new post do also offer a focus for newly promoted staff.

For those teachers moving to another school, joining the appraisal process is but one of many things to be learned as part of induction. Circular 12/91 indicated that in such a situation the appraisal process should start all over again. In practice it has been possible for an appraisee to move school and continue to work on their original focus, providing this has relevance in the new school. One of the greatest change areas is that of a move to deputy head or headteacher level. For deputy heads there is certainly a need for some awareness raising, if not training, on the differences between teacher appraisal and the appraisal of deputy heads, particularly in respect of the opportunity to have two appraisers.

The relationship between a teaching and a non-teaching role may be a focus point for deputies that would benefit from exploration. Deputies may also find themselves in the situation of working as an appraiser, managing the appraisal system and being INSET coordinator. This may already be the case for other members of staff, but managing these appraisal roles, as well as managing the post of deputy head, does offer a different dimension. We would suggest a half-day training awareness event could be offered for deputies or heads, by an LEA or group of schools working together, perhaps once or twice each year. This pattern is already in place in many LEAs. We would suggest that the programme shown opposite could be a useful guide.

For headteachers, the current pattern seems to be one day's training, where possible including LEA adviser/officer appraisers in the process.

A Possible Deputy/Heads Appraisal Course

0900   Aims, objectives, introductions
0915   The roles of a deputy head in terms of appraisal
0930   The Regulatory, DfEE and LEA requirements of appraisal
0945   Exploring the issues of appraisal for deputy heads. A
        thinking, question and answer session
1015   Feedback and answers to questions
1045   Refreshments
1100   Choosing a focus as a deputy head
1130   Reviewing the situation
1200   Final issues
1215   Close

TEACHERS RETURNING AFTER ABSENCE

For those teachers returning to school after a lengthy period of absence there will need to be both an introduction to the appraisal process and to the skills involved in making the process work. Training of this type is being offered by some LEAs on a needs basis, perhaps one session per term or less frequently, where appropriate. What is important for this group is that they are brought up to date with the current state of appraisal nationally, locally and in their own schools, and feel that they have the skills to fit into the process. The skills section later in this chapter may be helpful for such teachers.

AN OVERALL VIEW

As money is not now as available as it was for appraisal training it may be seen as more difficult to provide training for any of the groups we have identified, certainly in the way it has previously been provided. We are no longer starting from scratch when introducing everyone to the process and each school needs to decide on the priority it places on the appraisal process and how much emphasis is placed on training. As a result of this decision, other decisions can then be made as to how the training will be provided. INSET days provide the obvious opportunity, when small groups can work together, either within a school or bringing a number of schools together, but they are not the answer to everything. One solution being adopted by some schools is that the provision of training becomes part of the development of a member of staff who becomes a proficient trainer in their own right and becomes a resource which can then be 'sold' to other schools.

In looking towards training for the second cycle and beyond, there are key questions to ask:

- What is the specific need for training?
- What are the most appropriate ways of meeting these needs in order to provide the greatest cost benefit for both the individual teachers and the school as a whole?
- How is the training to be evaluated in terms of its effectiveness in ensuring that people can gain most from the process?

We would suggest that in the current climate using the experience and expertise of existing members of staff may well be a way of providing effective training. It is not suggested that this is imposed on people as an additional burden, rather that the provision of training becomes a part of the job of certain staff members. Money that may have been spent on training providers from outside school may well be channelled appropriately.

We would further suggest that whole staffs or departments review together the progress made in appraisal in the school as a way of training for the future. If it is to be a really meaningful exercise appraisal has to be related to the day-to-day work of those involved. If training can be related in the same context this may provide most value. From our experience there is no doubt that the need many appraisers have is in extended skills training. We therefore devote the rest of this chapter to this subject.

SKILLS TRAINING

Within the context of this book, and to assist in gaining the maximum benefit from any appraisal system, both appraisers and appraisees may need extended skills training. This will not only assist in the smooth running of any appraisal system but will improve communication skills, assist change and ensure the most valuable and productive outcomes for both the individual and the school in terms of staff and school development planning. We will discuss what we consider to be the major skills for appraisal, but these are obviously transferable in any interaction or communication within an organisation. The first step to effective interpersonal communication is relationship building.

Relationship building

There are many skills necessary to building effective relationships. Good relationships with both pupils and colleagues make teaching and learning more effective and enjoyable. They enable people to work together efficiently and cooperatively. Good relationships within an organisation help to develop a positive attitude and assist in change. We will concentrate on three areas of skills training which we believe to be fundamental in building effective relationships – respect, empathy and genuineness.

Respect

To have respect for someone means that you value them as an individual – their unique qualities – and that you think they are worthwhile. Showing respect for someone and valuing them as an individual is as an important a skill in terms of relationships with colleagues as it is in relationships with students. Respect has to be earned by our behaviour and cannot be demanded as a right. We convey respect in a number of ways. The following strategies work as well in the classroom as they do in the staff room or in the context of appraisal, and act as a simple guide to help build good relationships.

It is always encouraging to give positive attention to a person. This means not being distracted by other things when engaged in dialogue, as well as avoiding interrupting or talking over the other person. These strategies involve not only active listening but responding to things being said by a nod, a small interjection, a question or other encouragement to continue. This may take time, but giving time is the essence of valuing a person's contribution.

It is also important to remember that while it is advisable to be concerned with remembering the names of others it is also helpful to introduce yourself. In appraisal we believe that it is important that appraisers should spend some time in considering their job and introducing themselves to the appraisees in terms of how they see their job as an appraiser. After all, relationships are two way. These are basic courtesies alongside the usual Ps and Qs.

Empathy

Chambers Dictionary defines empathy as the 'power of entering into another's personality and imaginatively experiencing his experiences'. Although it now forms part of the National Curriculum requirements in History, and possibly should be included in other subject specifications, its importance in human relationships is obvious. If you can share related experiences of your own (after, of course, first acknowledging the relevance of the other person's experience) then you are drawing together in conveying empathy. If you can reflect the other person's feelings by smiling when the other person smiles or frowning in sympathy with the other person, or acknowledging their feelings by remarking 'You must be feeling tired' or 'Yes, you clearly sound happy', then you are doing a lot to enter into an effective and empathetic relationship. This is one of the most powerful and reassuring aspects of the appraisal process, no matter whether people are coming together for the first time or have a long-standing appraisal relationship.

Genuineness
The last, but not least, of our three key skills is the need to be genuine. We all know what it is like to meet someone that we feel is 'all things to all people', whom we feel not only 'runs with the hare' but also 'hunts with the hound'. This kind of relationship causes discomfort. There is a lack of trust. We feel that the person is hiding behind their role or putting up a facade, blocking any genuine or meaningful contact. We feel that we never get to know the real person, or that for some reason they do not wish us to know the real person. Such behaviour puts us on our guard and militates against constructive dialogue.

To convey a feeling of being genuine there are various behavioural indicators that we can encourage in ourselves that help to produce that trust. Being genuine is of as much concern to students as it is to adults. Students respond to people they like and therefore are predisposed to learn more effectively, just as adults will be more cooperative if other people are not pretending to be something they are not. Giving the impression of being genuine is no substitute. It is important to develop skills involving the ability to talk appropriately about oneself, the ability to share feelings appropriately, alongside the ability to behave in a non-verbal manner that is consistent with one's verbal behaviour. All these skills help to give the impression of genuine communication, but if you are still putting on an act, no one will believe you. If we are struggling to find time for appraisal then the least we can do is be genuine with each other.

Although effective relationships underlie all other communication skills there are a number of other key skills necessary throughout the process of appraisal. We will discuss the following:

- Negotiation
- Questioning
- Listening

- Feedback
- Recording
- Observation.

Negotiation

Throughout the appraisal process it will be necessary for both appraiser and appraisee to negotiate, ranging from negotiating the time and place for the initial meeting, the focus, time and place of the classroom observation, to the content of the statement and the setting of targets. These negotiations, we hope, bear little resemblance to the popularised and all too familiar types of negotiations related to pay bargaining or industrial disputes, although the skills involved are not dissimilar.

Much will depend on the relationship already established between the two people, the key element of which is trust, often absent in industrial dispute negotiations. In the context of appraisal, negotiation is seen to be a process of two people talking to reach an agreement, which is satisfactory to both the school and the individual and with which both parties agree. A process referred to as 'principled negotiation' was developed in America. It is designed to decide issues on their merits rather than through any form of 'haggling' or 'trading off'. This process implies that it is both possible and essential to look for mutual gains and can be successful in a number of ways.

Before any negotiation can take place it is essential that the appraisee and appraiser are clear not only about each other's roles in the process but also that the exchange is two way. If the process of negotiation is to be efficient and effective it should improve the relationship between the participants, as well as resulting in some beneficial decision. This can be achieved if we have the ability to separate the people from the problem.

Separate the people from the problem
People need to accept they are attacking a problem, not each other, and that they both bring to the process feelings, principles, prejudices, etc. It has to be accepted that negotiators are people first and space must be given for this. Human emotions can cloud rational judgements, misunderstanding can lead to confusion and resentment. During any negotiation ask yourself: Am I considering the person's feelings?

In doing this have some basic considerations:

- Use empathy, put yourself in their shoes.
- Don't make assumptions about their position.

- Don't blame the other person if the problem is yours.
- Check out and discuss each other's perceptions.
- Ensure equal participation.
- Make your verbal and non-verbal reactions consistent with each other.
- Recognise and understand emotions which may be displayed by yourself and the other person and be prepared to deal rationally with them.
- Allow both participants to let off steam.
- Use active listening skills genuinely.
- Ensure what you say is understood.

The basic approach must be to realise you are working with another person.

Focus on the interests of both people
What are the things within appraisal that concern both parties? These could be: ensuring the process works well and is intrinsically rewarding; whole school development; reassurances; a job well done and better use of resources.

In doing this have some basic considerations:

- Ask 'why' questions.
- Ask 'why not?'
- Examine which of possible multiple interests need exploration.
- Remember that without the satisfaction of basic human needs nothing will happen.
- Be enthusiastic.
- Look forward, not back – you can alter the future, not the past.

Generate a variety of options
Ensure that a variety of options are explored before coming to a final decision. These may be general or more specific and ought to come from both people. In some cases, there may be more options than others.

In doing this have some basic considerations:

- Work between specific and general options.
- Allow time for the options to be considered before a final decision is made.
- Obtain other opinions on options but do not break the confidentiality of the appraisal process.
- Have regard for answers that need resources.
- Identify preferences which may be useful to explore later.
- Look for consequences of... and consequences of not...

Questioning

The purpose of questioning in any interview situation is to encourage the person to talk, to feel free to express their ideas and opinions, with the interviewer in sufficient control to be able to probe or extend. Patterns of questioning tend to fall into two main categories, *recall* questions and *process* questions, with a number of questioning strategies available to elicit response. These two categories are fairly self-evident. *Recall* questions require the person to recall information from past experience. Opening devices range from such potentially closed questions as 'Did you enjoy your holiday?' to the more open approach of 'Tell me about...' *Process* questions ask a person to give an opinion, make judgements and offer an interpretation. They are, by the very nature of the response required, more open questions, ranging from 'What do you think about...?' to 'How would you cope with...?' Answers to *recall* questions often lead to an opportunity to ask a *process* question.

There are a variety of questioning strategies that can be adopted to illicit responses, including the open and closed methods already referred to. *Closed questions* are not always very productive if you wish a person to extend themselves or elaborate on information as they tend to encourage short, specific answers, often the monosyllabic reply of 'Yes' or 'No'. A succession of questions of this type will tend to sound like an interrogation rather than a discussion. However, they can be useful as a device to check facts or understanding, to gather specific information as a way of preparing to move forward to the next section or for bringing an interview to a close. *Leading questioning* techniques can have a similar effect, in that they too have a tendency to suggest a certain answer, or may influence the appraisee, as they often imply an opinion held by the appraiser, for example 'Surely you agree with the head's decision?' It is not the task of the interviewer to influence or express disapproval but to allow the other person to offer their own opinions and feelings. However, a closed question is useful to bring an interview to a close. The same effect can be achieved by using the technique of giving a brief *summary*. This is a useful device not only to close the interview but to check your understanding of a person's answer. A technique used by the more aggressive interviewer, and not often recommended is that of *confrontation*. However, it has its limited uses in that it allows one person to check the values held by the other.

Open questions that frequently begin with 'How' 'When' or 'Tell me about' are of much greater value when wishing to encourage a person to expand their ideas or offer their opinions and are a very useful technique to encourage confidence and trust. Another technique used in interviewing to encourage elaboration is that of asking the candidate to *reflect* on things that they referred to earlier, or that happened in the past. It is useful to use the person's own words to encourage them to give further information on a particular topic. These questions usually begin by suggesting that 'You said that...', thus encouraging the person to reflect and elaborate or reconsider. A *comparison* question is another very useful method of questioning for exploring attitudes and feelings. When wishing for more relevant information to be obtained it is often useful to pose a *hypothetical/theoretical* question as a person is then able to draw on past experience in order to give a clearer idea of their interests or capabilities. However, it is often a puzzling form of questioning for the person being interviewed and again weighs heavily with the time factor. Do we really have time to be hypothetical? More can probably be learned by asking what the person actually 'did' rather than speculating on what they 'might have done'. Theoretical questions are only likely to give an indication of the person's behaviour. Many individuals are good at giving theoretical answers to questions about what they 'would do', but often those who do not know the textbook answer are excellent in 'real life' situations. It is, therefore, far better to ask *behavioural* questions than hypothetical/theoretical types.

Finally, there is often no more powerful a question than *silence*.

Patterns of questioning
As well as different types of questioning there are also different patterns of questioning. A good technique is to *funnel* questions where the appraiser starts with a very general, open-ended question such as 'Tell me about...? A good follow-up technique is to funnel the questions through four stages, starting with the general 'Tell me about' the situation, moving on to more detail about the task and person's role or responsibility in that situation. The next step is to funnel into the action that was taken, 'How did you go about it?', and finally to talk about the result or outcomes of that situation.

A similar pattern of questioning but one that starts from the closed, more specific type of question and moves to the open, more general type is referred to as the *pyramid* pattern. This method can be used with a person to concentrate the mind during an interview.

Two other patterns of questioning that are often adopted in a more formal interview situation are those of the *tunnel* and those referred to as *erratic* questioning patterns. The tunnel pattern is when a set of preset questions are given to all interviewees and the answers form the criteria for the assessment. This can be a useful tool to use when wishing to compare a number of people, but is not useful for appraisal where the process is individual. The erratic form of questioning is self-explanatory and offers no particular pattern. This type of questioning tends to cause confusion and stress and is not recommended in an appraisal situation.

Following are some suggestions of questions to use for an appraisal review. These can be used by the appraisee and appraiser as a preparation base for an interview. In the 'real' situation the questions could be tailored for each individual teacher or school. It is envisaged that the appraisee would think through the questions as a self-appraisal, the appraiser would then explore the questions further with the appraisee in the review session. The questions are structured so as to allow use by two people working on a training course. The purpose of the exercise is structured practice in the review technique which underlies the whole appraisal process. We would not of course suggest that all the questions are used or that they are asked in turn.

A Suggested Pattern of Questions

From the past
What prompted you to work with the age group or subject you teach at present?
What experiences have you found most fulfilling in this work?
Have you always taught this subject or age group?
Who has influenced you most in your work?
Tell me about the highlights of your work in the past.
What have you got out of your work over the past term or year?
What haven't you got from it which you expected?
What do you feel are your major successes?
What have you done to develop areas you feel you are weak in?
Have you sought advice of any kind?
Did the advice help?
Were you able to act on it?

The present
What do you like about the job at present?
Do you have a specific role in the school?
How do you feel about this role?
Do you have a job description?
Do you feel satisfied that it covers all your duties?
How has the description been arrived at?
Does the description simply describe what you should do, or does it profile your job in an active way?
What frustrations do you feel in your present post?
Do you feel you are part of a team?

How do you feel the team works together?
How do you feel about the time you have to do your job?
Do you feel you have all the resources you need to work effectively and efficiently?
What do you feel are the conflicts within your role?
How do you feel others in school perceive you?
What changes do you feel are needed in school?
How do you feel you can be involved in these changes?
Do you feel your teaching/management style could be shared with others?
Are you happy with your style?
How do you feel about record keeping in school?
How do you feel you can be involved in these changes?
Do you feel your teaching/management style could be shared with others?
How do you evaluate your performance?
What is most satisfying to you about your job at present?
What support do you feel you receive?
What support would you like to receive and from whom?
Do you feel the school system restricts your development?

The future
What do you want for yourself from your job and the school?
What contribution do you feel you would like to make to the school?
What would you like the school to offer you next year?
What plans have you made for the next year?
How do you hope to achieve your plans?
How will you know you have achieved them?
What are your immediate training needs for the future?
Is there anything specifically you wish to do next year?
What INSET do you wish to see next year?
Do you feel you would like to take on any extra responsibilities?
How can the school help you achieve your personal goals?
What can I do to help you?
What can others do to help you?
Where do you think you are going in your professional life?
What can you do to help yourself achieve your goals?
Have you thought about where you do or do not want to be in five years' time?
What specific actions do you wish to take: now; next term; next year?

If you have asked at least some of these questions you will need to do a lot of listening to the answers.

Figure 5.1 *Suggested questions for use in an appraisal review*

Listening

Questioning and listening skills are complementary. A good inter-viewer will not only ask the appropriate questions but will also listen carefully to the replies. Without the listening the interview will grind to an embarrassing close. There are several elements to bear in mind when conducting any interview. A good interviewer will:

- concentrate on the responses to questions;
- probe to seek necessary additional information;
- use questions to clarify points;
- summarise;
- make effective use of non-verbal signals.

The appraisee should leave the interview feeling that it has been fair, friendly and efficient. Each stage of questioning involves good listening. Let us take the funnel pattern of questioning as an example. Here we start with a general, open-ended question. The interview can then only proceed with careful, attentive listening in order to follow-up with a probe or paraphrase of the initial outline. Only when you listen carefully can you check for understanding or clarification of any factual detail. When the interviewer is clear about the facts the interview can be moved into the area of feelings and motivations. Again, listening is a crucial skill, for only when you are sure that things have been understood can a summary and confirmation of ideas occur.

Most people spend more time listening than they spend on any other communication activity; however, a large number of people never learn to listen effectively. They develop poor listening habits that tend to continue throughout their lives and which, unless they are careful, get passed on to others.

The first principle to conducting a good interview is to try to find an appropriate setting, one where there is a degree of privacy and little likelihood of interruption. While we appreciate that the ideal setting is difficult to achieve in the midst of hectic teaching commitments, and that often negotiation is carried out in the corridor or on break duty, we feel that it is beneficial to both parties if the surroundings can be more conducive to calm and relative tranquillity. There are no regulations which say appraisal discussions have to take place on school premises – the licensed trade in fact is doing quite well out of appraisal! A setting either facilitates or hinders the process and, therefore, the outcomes. The setting arranged for any part of the appraisal process that involves listening should be non-threatening and conducive to conversation. Maybe the head's office is not the most appropriate, even if there is one. There are a number of things that can be tried to achieve a good working relationship.

Privacy
As far as possible ensure an atmosphere of privacy. Distractions should be avoided. It is easy for a person's concentration to waiver if the phone is constantly ringing or if people are walking in and out of the room demanding attention. If people are standing or sitting within earshot this too can be distracting. Therefore:

- Close the door.
- Take the phone off the hook.
- Leave a 'Do not disturb' notice on the door. However, this does not help if there are young children in the school who cannot read!

Eliminate barriers
An appraisal interview differs from a job interview in that, although there is negotiation, your future salary does not depend on it. If the outcome of the interview is going to be beneficial to both the individual and the school it is worth taking the time to set up an easy atmosphere to achieve this. A desk may be seen as a symbol of power. As well as acting on a simple physical level as a barrier, it also acts on the psychological level as a more subtle barrier. A desk can signal the message of superiority. As a symbol of power the owner implies that they have the right to sit at it and pass judgement. Therefore, whether the classroom or the head's office becomes the interview room, it is advisable to organise a suitable alternative seating arrangement by changing the position of the chairs and desks to avoid this subtle power imbalance. However, if both people are happy that the desk is not a barrier, but a good place to put papers, then use it.

Use of surroundings
Once you have organised the seating to suit the desired atmosphere of equality necessary in an appraisal interview it is also advisable for both participants to sit at the same level. There are parallel psychological messages of power implied if one seat is higher than another or if one person has an easy chair and the other has a hard, upright chair. This can be particularly relevant in primary schools where the chairs for the pupils are considerably lower than chairs of normal height. It is also more conducive to attentive listening if people are not only at the same level but, rather than facing each other, are at right angles. This avoids the discomfort of sitting in what may be seen as a confrontational, 'face-to-face' style.

Barriers to good listening

If there are too many distractions of noise, the movement of people, or anything demanding attention, then there is a tendency for what is referred to as *hubbub listening*. If there is a general atmosphere of 'hubbub' then neither party will be able to concentrate fully, however hard they try. Another pitfall is that most of us tend to think about four times more quickly than we can speak, so the listener has three-quarters of a minute of spare thinking time for each listening minute. This means that sometimes we allow our minds to be distracted by our own concerns or preoccupations. This habit of listening is referred to as *on-off listening* or *not paying attention*.

Appearing to be *glassy-eyed* is allied to the barrier of on-off listening. This is when we think we are giving the appearance of paying careful attention to the other person but our minds are on other things and in other places. We have a dreamy, far-away look in our eyes. We have witnessed it in others so can be sure that others will recognise it in us, especially when we are tired or preoccupied. It can act as an insult to the other person as it implies boredom or disinterest and is a habit to be avoided. Another type of barrier to attentive listening is *pseudo listening*. This is when an interviewer has developed the ability to give the impression of careful attention while avoiding the glassy-eyed pitfall. Nevertheless, interest was lost after the first few sentences and the mind has gone to pastures new.

Other pitfalls to concentrated listening centre not around outside physical distractions and tiredness but on some of our own psychological 'baggage' that we bring with us to the interview, which can act as a blocking device when listening to another person. One particular blocking mechanism is referred to as *red flag listening*, taking its name because some words are like the proverbial 'red rags to a bull'. For some it may be the topic being discussed that enrages their sensibilities, for others it may simply be that the person speaking uses too much jargon, or speech littered with unexplained acronyms. Whatever the reason, when this happens we stop listening. We tune them out. We *rehearse* what we will say and wait for an opportunity to say it. Closely allied to this is that we do not like to have our own pet ideas, prejudices or points of view overturned. Consequently, when another person says something that appears to clash with what we think or believe, unconsciously, as a defence mechanism, we may either stop listening altogether or begin to prepare our own counter-attack. The habits of *defensive listening* or *listening for points of disagreement* are occasions where the listener seems to wait for a moment of confrontation and follows it up in either defensive or attacking mode.

Other poor listening habits or barriers to good listening are known as *matter over mind listening,* where our ears are open but our mind is closed. This is when we are too ready to jump to conclusions. We feel we are capable of predicting what the other person will say. When this happens we decide that there is no reason to listen further as we feel we know what they are about to say and will hear nothing new. This tendency to decide too quickly that either the subject or the speaker are predictable or boring is called *open ears – closed mind listening.*

It is also useful to avoid being *subject centred* rather than *speaker centred.* Sometimes we concentrate on the problem and not the person. If we allow the details and facts of an incident to become more important than what people are saying about themselves, we are in danger of not picking up on some of the more subtle subtext and will lose valuable opportunities for constructive feedback.

Often, when we wish to avoid forgetting what has taken place in an interview, and because it would be counter-productive to take in a tape recorder, we try to put down on paper everything that has been said. This is known as *pencil listening.* If we try to do this we are bound to lose some of what has been said. Few of us are skilled in shorthand, but even so the spoken word is far faster than the written word. Pencil listening also has another huge disadvantage in that while a person is writing their head is down. This reduces eye contact and tends to make people feel you are uninterested in what they are saying. For the person talking it is rather like talking into a vacuum, similar to a telephone conversation, where all nuances of body language are missed and misunderstandings often occur.

Body language is obviously a very important part of developing listening skills. Interpreting non-verbal signals and what they imply are subtle skills that need to be considered. Adequate eye contact is one of the most important ways of communicating full and undivided attention, as shown by the example of pencil listening.

Eye contact
The key words here are 'adequate' and 'appropriate'. It is advisable that continuous eye contact is avoided, as this can be interpreted as staring and can make a person feel uncomfortable. Just as discomforting is to feign eye contact by fixing the gaze on the person's forehead. Both these types of non-verbal behaviour can suggest hostility or insincerity. Similarly, it is disconcerting to feel that someone is staring, or is being constantly distracted by people walking past or other extraneous noises. To reassure a person that they have your full attention avoid looking away for any length of

time. However, the key to eye contact is to be as natural as possible and strike a balance between appearing to stare and appearing uninterested.

Other non-verbal gestures involve *head nodding* occasionally to affirm attention, the *use of silence* to communicate patience and the use of appropriate *facial gestures,* which should reflect the other person's expressed feelings and not your reactions to them. A frown can be appropriate when a person's point was not understood. It is a valuable, non-verbal gesture, suggesting the need for clarification or elaboration.

Body language involves the use of the whole body and not simply the face. If one person displays an *open body posture* it signals and encourages the other person to relax. An open body posture shows receptivity and encourages the other person to talk freely and be less defensive. Open body postures can be achieved by, for example, avoiding crossed arms as this can act as a barrier and signal defensiveness or superiority. Also avoid slouching or an overly 'laid back' attitude as this can signal a lack of interest or tiredness.

Bodies are great communicators. In our culture we tend to rely heavily on both giving and receiving messages from the words that are spoken and the tone of voice they are spoken in. While these are the more obvious methods of direct communication, the body can communicate in a language that signals the more subtle nuances of encouragement or hostility. It is important to be aware of both the barriers and the encouragements to good listening techniques.

Having said all this we believe that a good dose of common sense will make listening a useful process, too much concentration on trying to listen in the 'right' way can cause more problems than it is worth.

Feedback

Since this is a guide for both appraisers and appraisees it would be useful in this section to discuss both *giving feedback* and *receiving feedback.* Constructive feedback is an excellent way not only to learn about ourselves but also to learn about the effect we have on others. Constructive feedback can increase self-awareness and offer ideas to encourage development. However, constructive feedback does not always imply positive feedback, although this should be the first option. Negative feedback, if given sensitively and skilfully, is just as important to self-development. Negative feedback does not necessarily imply destructive feedback. Destructive feedback is when negative feedback is given in an unskilled way, leaving the person feeling inadequate but with nothing to build on and without suggestions for development.

Giving feedback

There are a number of constructive, helpful ideas to bear in mind when giving feedback. Teachers were all taught in college, and this was reinforced on teaching practice, the importance of giving students or pupils *positive* feedback first. So it is with adults. This allows for encouragement and recognition of the things that we do well. Begin by saying what you liked about an aspect of the observation or what you thought had been done well. Avoid listing the mistakes that were made, as this can block our appreciation of the strengths of the other person. If the positive is registered first, any negative feedback is more likely to be accepted and acted upon. When giving feedback try to be *specific*. Avoid general comments as they are not very helpful when it comes to developing skills. It is of little value to offer a vague comment that the person was 'wonderful' without referring to the specific action or ability that led to the comment being made. Specific feedback allows greater opportunity for personal development.

It is also useful to *refer only to behaviour that can be changed*. A person cannot change the way they look, but they can modify the impact their behaviour has on others. It is, therefore, not helpful to say that you don't like a person's face, whereas it can be helpful if you suggest that, for you, it would help if they tried to smile a little more. This means that you are *offering alternatives* by turning the negative into a positive suggestion. When giving feedback it is important not to imply any value judgements. *Be descriptive* in your comments rather than *evaluative*, by telling the person the effect that their actions had on you. Again avoid the over-general 'that was good' comment, but give a specific example of behaviour and the effect it had on you. At all times in appraisal, when giving feedback, use examples and descriptive evidence – it brings the situation alive.

Since feedback says as much about the giver as the receiver it is a useful learning experience for both parties. If we listen to the feedback that we give it will indicate to us our own values and what we tend to focus on in others. It is important that we *take responsibility for the feedback* that we give. If we begin with 'In my opinion' we avoid giving the impression of being 'the font of all knowledge'. We are only able to give our experience of that person at that particular time and must avoid appearing to offer some kind of universally agreed opinion related to that individual. Skilled feedback offers people information about themselves in a way that leaves them with a choice about whether to act on it or not and helps to examine the consequences of any decision related to change. It does not involve prescribing change.

Receiving feedback
Feedback can be uncomfortable to hear but it is helpful and polite *to listen* rather than immediately to reject it or argue about it. Remember that others do have perceptions related to our behaviour and it can be useful to be aware of these. Having listened to their feedback you, as an individual, are free to accept or reject those conclusions, feeling them to be irrelevant or of little significance as far as you are concerned. But make sure you *understand the feedback* before you respond to it. It is all too easy to jump to conclusions or be on the defensive. A useful way, as in an interview situation, is to offer a summary of what you believe has been said. This avoids jumping to conclusions when they are not applicable. *Check it out with others.* Avoid relying on one source of information which, after all, only forms one person's perception of your behaviour or attitude. Often other people's perceptions differ. If we ask more than one person it helps us to arrive at a more balanced conclusion and keeps any feedback in proportion. If we get feedback on some aspect of our behaviour and not others which are of concern to us personally then it is useful to *ask the appraiser* to cover any aspects that you feel have not been addressed.

For personal development it is important to know how others experience us and we can use feedback to help in our development. When we receive feedback we assess its value within the relationship and context of its generation. We assess the consequences of taking it seriously or ignoring it. This will differ greatly and is dependent on the personal relationship between the appraiser and the appraisee. This, in turn, is directly related to how much trust and communication has been developed beforehand. After the feedback, however, it is up to the individual to decide how, if at all, to modify their behaviour.

Recording
The recording of information is an activity that occurs at all stages of the appraisal cycle. An individual may wish to record information in an informal manner during the self-appraisal process. Some form of recording is necessary during the observation and data collection phases of appraisal, which leads to the more formal recording of the final written statement and target setting.

In the initial stages of the appraisal process it is useful to have some form of record related to self-appraisal. This can mean using a variety of prompt sheets, examples of which have been given in Chapter 1. Record keeping at this stage in the process can be extended into a more comprehensive analysis of a person's current role in the school and any future ambitions or targets. It is also useful to record any thoughts related to possible areas of focus for the observation. Other types of prompt sheets suggest areas of concern under different headings and encourage the individual to enter more details about their activities. Whichever method is chosen some form of written record is more useful than relying on memory.

At the initial meeting, where arrangements are being made for the observation, it is desirable that both parties record any agreements reached. The purpose of the initial meeting is to look at the person's job description, to agree the timetable and scope of the appraisal, to identify the area of focuses, to agree arrangements for classroom observation and to agree any other methods of data collection necessary to complete the process. It is beneficial if both participants have kept some form of record of the agreements reached related to those areas.

Even if a formal record related to self-appraisal has not been kept, and only a perfunctory record on the agreements reached of the arrangements for the observation, it is imperative that some form of recording is undertaken during the actual classroom observation. It is also necessary to keep records related to any other forms of data collection. This evidence will be needed later to form the basis of the interview, and to assist in any staff development programme. The method and style of record keeping for the observation need to be agreed beforehand and both parties need to be clear about what is being observed and how it is to be recorded. Some schools favour prompt sheets of agreed competencies while others leave the form of the recording to the individuals involved.

Whichever method of recording is favoured it is useful to have agreed on some performance indicators. It might help to have addressed these questions beforehand:

- What do I wish to achieve? TARGET
- What do I need to help me? STRATEGY
- What or whom do I need to help me? RESOURCES
- How do I know my progress? PERFORMANCE INDICATORS
- When will this be achieved by? TIME SCALE

If all these questions have been effectively answered this will serve as an adequate record to enable the achievement of targets. Figure 1.8 in Chapter 1 serves this purpose well.

The first stage of the appraisal process is complete when an agreed statement has been written by the appraiser. This is the most formal record of the process and can be written at the end of the interview by both the appraiser and the appraisee. However, what usually tends to happen is that the appraiser takes away the notes related to the interview and composes a statement that is then agreed by both parties.

The minimum statement needs to provide an accurate record of the main points discussed during the interview, the conclusions reached and the professional development targets agreed. The length of the statements varies considerably. This formal record can be very time consuming, especially for the conscientious appraiser who wishes to do the best for a colleague. There are no easy answers to this dilemma.

Finally, some schools have devised a form of record keeping that encompasses the whole of the process and enables both participants to keep a useful organisational record of its time scale. Having a record of the key dates and times of the components in the process acts as a useful safety mechanism in otherwise overcrowded timetables.

A useful summary might look like Figure 5.2.

Timetable Summary		
STAGE	**DATE**	**NOTES**
Initial meeting		
Data collection		
Observation 1		
Observation 2		
Feedback meeting		
Interview		
Follow-up meeting(s)		
Statement		
Review meeting		

Figure 5.2 *Example of written record of appraisal time scale*

Observation
Observation has been discussed in detail in Chapter 1 but in terms of training we would like to add the following comments.

We believe that objectivity is extremely difficult, if not impossible to achieve, given that both colleagues will have prior knowledge of each other's work. However, if the criteria for the observation have been agreed then it is the job of the observer to provide evidenced examples to illustrate their findings. In this way a measure of objectivity can be built into the process. Comments made by the observer without supported examples are relatively useless if the purpose of observation is to feed back what actually happened in the classroom.

One of the major criticisms related to observation is that it involves the observer in making interpretations of data. We suggest more use is made of video or audio recording. If these devices are used both parties can replay the observation at a later date and discuss their interpretations of the sequence and effects of that particular lesson.

Some people will argue that observation is a highly developed scientific activity and that the vast majority of teachers do not have the experience or training to carry out classroom observation in this way. Indeed Paul Oliver, in his article 'Quality in the Classroom' (1992), discusses the 'enormously complex and sophisticated infrastructure for judging the standards of teaching' and questions the validity of the 'judgements' made in the assessment of teacher effectiveness through the observation process.

All teachers constantly engage in observation of pupils in their everyday work, using highly developed skills in both observation and communication. All we ask is that teachers apply the same criteria to each other in appraisal observation; however, some teachers are more competent at these activities than others. Where this is the case, training may be needed as part of the teacher's professional development.

There are many opportunities available for teachers to develop their observation skills, in both formal and informal situations, ranging from popping into a classroom to collect some materials to the more formal appraisal observation or to observation as part of a pre-school inspection exercise.

To help raise the standard and effectiveness of appraisal observation the following checklist can be used as a basis for a training exercise:

- Ensure appraiser and appraisee understand and agree why observation is taking place.
- Ensure both participants understand exactly what is being observed.
- Establish clear ground rules for how and when the appraiser enters the classroom and what they will do, once in the classroom.

- Establish clear understanding of what is to be achieved in the lesson observed.
- Establish clear performance indicators to determine success during the lesson against which the appraiser can collect evidence.
- Ensure that the role of the appraiser is clearly understood by both the participants and the pupils.
- Establish a practical, appropriate method for recording information during the observation.
- Feedback should be based only on evidence collected in the classroom, not on the appraiser's view of what should have happened.

It may be useful as a training exercise, before observation takes place, for the appraiser and appraisee to watch a section of video that has filmed a lesson in progress and jointly conduct a simulated observation exercise. The training observation could start with both participants watching the video lesson, making notes on what they saw and their perception of the effectiveness of the activity and then comparing notes. Through discussion the participants can refine their observation notes. In this way both can agree to have the same focus in the lesson, replay the video and concentrate on observing only the agreed focus. Again notes can be compared. Both participants should now be able to agree criteria for observation in a lesson and design a form of recording to match this which could then be used. By working through this process appraiser and appraisee enhance their working relationship and sharpen their observation skills. This is increased even further if the video is of a lesson that has taken place in their own school. Feedback and discussion can then take place with the actual teacher being seen on the video. This, of course, depends on time and the goodwill of the teacher involved.

IN CONCLUSION

Training needs can only be identified by the people engaged in the process and this implies that they recognise a need. Without this recognition any form of training can be ineffective. Training needs will be determined by a coherent staff development policy, drawn up in conjunction with ongoing consultations with staff. Only in this way can appraisal move forward to embrace the model of continuing professional development. In this process, individuals recognise and acknowledge their own training and developmental needs, and the cycle really does become 360°.

6

Appraisal for All

We have made clear throughout this book that we believe appraisal must be integrated into the school development plan and become a cornerstone of staff development policy. Every school we have come into contact with is striving to become more effective and to offer every member of its community the opportunity to really be part of a learning organisation. This does not mean we believe every person may want to be a part! In our terms a learning organisation means a number of things:

- All people in the organisation are given the opportunity to learn naturally while they are working and are supported in doing so by structured, well-managed processes and systems which enable people to learn in a variety of ways.
- Everyone is able to engage in a review process which is clearly aimed at identifying their developmental needs and how these can be met along with meeting those of the organisation. This process provides the opportunity for giving and receiving constructive feedback on performance.
- The organisation is clearly, publicly and visibly committed to valuing learning for all, as a significant way of achieving its objectives.
- The organisation clearly, publicly and visibly values learning for its own sake.
- All people in the organisation are easily able continuously to manage change for the benefit of all members of their organisation.

Many schools are already well on the road to becoming learning organisations as described above. However, some schools are also struggling to become learning organisations for all, ie all employees and all pupils. The first group of employees we will consider are the newly qualified teachers.

NEWLY QUALIFIED TEACHERS

The DfEE, in its memorandum 2/92, stated that 'teachers appointed on or after 1 September 1992 are no longer required to serve a probationary year'. It also stated that since newly qualified teachers will not now be known as probationary teachers but will be covered by the definition 'school teacher': 'LEAs and schools will wish to consider amending their schemes of appraisal so as to take account of the extension of appraisal to newly appointed teachers.' It further stressed, in this document, its commitment to expenditure on improvements in the induction of newly qualified teachers. It stated that its objectives in supporting expenditure by LEAs was to encourage 'the development of profiling and competence based approaches to professional development'. In our experience this seems to be the trend that is being developed in most schools.

Much work is being done to develop competence based approaches to the initial teaching and subsequent professional development of teachers. This is being done through the partnerships that already exist between providers of initial training and schools. Figure 6.1 is an example of practice devised by a mentor for a newly qualified teacher in a Northumberland school. It amalgamates ideas very similar to the prompt sheet examples seen earlier in this book, particularly those for self-appraisal and lesson observation. It also combines teacher competence models used in initial teaching training. This lesson evaluation prompt sheet has since been adopted by the school's partnership university. The university believed it to be an excellent and manageable working model and is now using this approach with all their partnership schools.

The continuing professional development of newly qualified teachers is an extension of this liaison between universities and schools. The professional development of the newly qualified teacher must be seen in terms of a working partnership between the individual teacher and the school themselves. To facilitate this approach most schools are devising comprehensive induction programmes for newly qualified teachers. One high school in Northumberland provides an excellent example where the staff development team have been working on a carefully constructed programme of induction and staff development. The same principles and features of any good induction scheme apply to all those entering teaching or adjusting to a new or different teaching culture. However, the content and length of induction will vary according to individual needs and the priorities of the school.

This school's aims are not dissimilar to those of any appraisal document:

> For the newly qualified teacher, a carefully planned and extended period of staff development is thought to be important. We aim to provide teacher support and guidance for the newly qualified teacher, professional coaching on the job, time to discuss issues of importance or concern, time to reflect, evaluate and offer praise and encouragement as well as personal and career development within a carefully planned staff development programme. This will include in-service training for professional review and development. Newly qualified teachers will have their first review in the summer of the first year.

This school has clearly stated that the first formal professional review, or appraisal, for newly qualified teachers will take place at the end of their first year of teaching. The review will be a compilation of all aspects of mentoring and evaluation of progress and development that have taken place throughout the year.

The newly qualified teacher has particular needs in progressing from initial training to a fully accountable professional status. The mentor or teacher allocated the responsibility for their staff development is an active partner in this development and shares responsibility for planning and evaluating the quality of dialogue and learning. The mentor can be seen as a surrogate appraiser for the initial induction of any newly qualified teacher.

The role of appraiser or assessor sometimes causes concern among teachers who also act as mentors, as it may be felt that the role of an assessor sits uncomfortably with the role of a mentor and trusted professional friend. It is therefore often seen to be the role of the manager, rather than the mentor, to engage in the more formal appraisal and feedback on work performance as an assessor, while the role of mentor is seen to be one of offering support for personal development, encouragement and confidential dialogue.

This conflict of roles occurs because the majority of teachers perform a significant part of their job without the presence of other members of staff. Observation can, therefore, be seen as an event rather than a continual two-way process. This clear distinction does not exist in the primary sector, or in first and middle schools, where teachers rely more on frequent informal contact, team teaching and joint planning. Some schools, particularly in the secondary sector, find it practical to split the roles of non-judgemental supporter or mentor and those of assessor or manager to avoid some of these difficulties.

Lesson Evaluation

Student Teacher: **Observation by:**

Date: **Time:**   **Class:**

Guidelines

The university requires us to comment on the following competencies during lesson observations. Reference to these competencies can be made under the following headings, but tutors will also need to make subject-specific comments.

Organisation of lesson

Coherent/relevant lesson plans	
Clear continuity/ progression	
Appropriate expectations	
Appropriate organisation of class/groups etc	

Teaching techniques used

Appropriate range of strategies	
Clear language/ stimulating material	
Appropriate resources, including use of IT	
Awareness of individual needs	

continued

Class control and discipline	
Creates and maintains orderly environment	
Appropriate rewards/sanctions	
Maintains motivation	

Subject-specific comments

Areas for development

Additional comments

Figure 6.1 *Example of mentor's evaluation sheet for a newly qualified teacher*

In these cases the school identifies roles for two different colleagues. The mentors undertake formative assessment to support professional development. They listen, interpret, enable, guide and validate evaluation. The mentor's evaluation will concentrate on the teacher's progress and development. The managerial role, whether curriculum leader or headteacher, also involves listening, advising and collaborative planning. Nevertheless the manager is the person identified as having the role of formal assessor, whose evaluation concentrates on the quality of teaching and learning of the pupils as well as the continuing development of the teacher. Where there is a split in the role of assessor and mentor, the mentor and the teacher can prepare and present together a shared statement of achievements and targets to the assessor. This statement informs any formal assessment procedures in operation in the school. These approaches can be seen as modifications of existing practice surrounding good appraisal and contain all the necessary components discussed for the appraisal cycle and staff development.

The school and the teacher will enter into a partnership of responsibility for the quality of induction and staff development. The teacher will invest time and effort in professional development in the form of self-evaluation and target setting, a process that is familiar, having already been practised during initial teacher training. The teacher, through self-appraisal and evaluation, will be able to provide feedback for both the mentor and curriculum leader to enable them, in turn, to support effectively.

The concept of an initial meeting to begin the appraisal process does not apply in quite the same way to newly qualified teachers. Frequent meetings are obviously inherent in the relationship between the mentor and the teacher. It makes good sense to start the induction process with a professional discussion of strengths, weaknesses and opportunities. All new teachers brings their own competencies and qualities. These qualities need to be valued and used if a genuine partnership of development for both the school and the individual is to be achieved. Depending on the style of the school this initial discussion may lead to a written set of targets or plans of action. However, it seems more general practice to leave formal target setting until the end of the first year or when the teacher enters the formal appraisal structure. It is then seen as a natural progression from the good practice established during the teacher's induction year.

During the first year of teaching, a programme of formal and informal meetings between the mentor and the teacher will be arranged, as will a timetable of observations. The interviewing that takes place following an observation in the formal appraisal cycle is provided for, during induction, as an ongoing support system between mentor and teacher. During this period of induction and development the mentor will encourage a pattern of self-evaluation and target setting by the teacher which is validated and supported by the mentor. The mentor also provides regular feedback throughout the year and a review towards the end of the first year of the teacher's achievements and progress through this induction period. It is simple then, as an extension of these interviews, for the first focus in the formal appraisal to be discussed and negotiated with the mentor, arising from the teacher's first year's experience.

Once a regular pattern of meetings and observations has been established it is important to ensure that these observations are useful and do not simply consist of 'walking past' or 'informal chats'. It is a good idea for all the lessons observed to be documented with a note of points arising. These can then be addressed in the discussions that follow and any decisions taken can be recorded by both the mentor and the teacher.

Most schools will find that a programme of induction will blend comfortably with the appraisal process. The good practices established during this period will be invaluable in maintaining a partnership between the newly qualified teacher and the school. The needs of the school will be fulfilled by the teacher, whose own needs will in turn be recognised by the school.

INVESTORS IN PEOPLE STANDARD

An ever-increasing number of schools are becoming committed to the Investors in People Standard. This offers a framework to ensure that all employees are given the opportunity for training and development and that this is delivered, reviewed and evaluated. A key part of the IIP process is that all employees have a regular opportunity for reviewing their development needs and that a process for reviewing exists. Three questions frequently asked by schools are:

1. Does the teacher appraisal process cover the needs of IIP in offering a review of development needs?
2. How do we extend this process to all staff?
3. How do we turn a review process into a fundamental part of a learning organisation?

1. Does the teacher appraisal process cover the needs of IIP?

The answer to the first question is yes, providing that the aims of appraisal as specified in the Regulations and Circular 12/91 are met. This only applies to teachers and not to other staff.

2. How do we extend this process to all staff?

The answer to the second question ought not to be a great problem in a school where the climate of a learning organisation is established. We see no reason why the framework of the teacher appraisal scheme cannot be applied to those staff who do not teach, as we discussed in Chapter 4. 'Ah,' people say, 'but what about classroom observation?' Again we make the point that classroom observation is basically about observing the teacher at work in the core element of their job. So why can you not have observation of someone else at work in the core element of their job? 'But teacher appraisal is compulsory' is the reply, 'we would not have classroom observation if it was not'. We think this is an arguable point and that where classroom observation has proved to have benefits for teachers, either in terms of teaching and learning or in other areas, observation may well be maintained even if not compulsory.

The average time being taken for a teacher appraisal, over the first year of the two-year cycle, is about three to five hours. We suggest that the time taken for an appraisal of support staff could reflect the complexity of their job and perhaps the time for which they are employed. It could be argued that the length of time taken for teacher appraisal is indicative of its worth to those involved and their level of comfort with the process. We cannot presume that because someone has a non-teaching function they should necessarily be entitled to less time.

Time is always the issue, but let's go back to the features of a learning organisation we indicated at the start of this chapter. If we really believe that this is the type of organisation we want then time has to be found for the processes to support people's learning. If positive, tangible benefits result in fewer mistakes, greater motivation, more effective schools, improved teaching and learning methods, then the time spent is worthwhile.

Who will the appraisers be? Who are the appraisers of teachers? Those who are deemed to have the ability, experience and credibility to carry out the function. When teacher appraisal began there were schools where only the headteacher and deputy were seen as fit to appraise. It is ironic that in some of those schools the headteacher and deputy were often seen by everyone else as unfit to appraise!

Things have changed. In many schools being an appraiser has been the epitome of learning naturally while at work. Many appraisers have said how much they have learned through their work as an appraiser: about themselves, their teaching and learning, and about the way they operate as part of the school organisation. One effect of this has been to encourage an ever-wider number of staff to become appraisers without diluting the efficacy of the process.

There is little reason why the same principle cannot be applied to support staff. Many support staff may neither wish to be appraisers nor feel themselves capable of undertaking the work. In this situation, which is fully understandable, there are two options. One is for members of the teaching staff to take on the role for those staff with whom they work closely, or for appraisal for non-teaching staff to be voluntary. Many teachers would, with justification, see the duty of appraising non-teaching staff as an imposition on already overcrowded time. Where this was the case such teachers should not be asked to undertake the work. Other teachers would see the appraisal as a formalisation of something they already did, and an opportunity of helping a colleague gain some greater value in their job. We are reminded here of one teacher who provided a review system for two nursery nurses she worked with, within that operated in the school for teachers before appraisal. The teacher claimed that the nursery nurses felt far more an equal part of the school's development by having their review alongside the teaching staff, a claim supported by the nursery nurses themselves.

One of the major results of appraisal is that of departmental or team improvement where appraisal has been undertaken as part of a departmental or team activity. On a number of occasions each member of a department has chosen to focus on an aspect of work identified as a priority by members of the department. We have been told repeatedly of the benefits this has brought to a department in terms of improved communications, consistency of approach, more efficient use of materials and resources, to name but a few. In most cases the issue of how to include non-teaching staff has been raised. The answer seems simple: include the staff in the appraisal process, but this solution may be complicated by, for example, budget and time implications. We must go back to first principles. What is the department about? What is it really trying to achieve? If the answer is that it is trying to maximise the effort in teaching and learning for all, then there really are no arguments. Time and financial budgets must reflect ways of achieving the overall aims. If this means providing a review or appraisal system for all, then cost-benefit analyses should be conducted to determine how this can best happen.

3. How do we turn a review process into a fundamental part of a learning organisation?

It is through all staff and pupils feeling that learning is a natural part of their activity at work that real progress towards a learning organisation can be made. At a time when budget cuts have forced staff redundancies and increased class sizes, such arguments may seem unrealistic. We would not deny that resources first and foremost have to be used to ensure adequate staffing for a realistic class size. Once this has been done it is vital that what remaining resources there are utilised to the benefit of all. Is it too simplistic to argue that a way of doing this is to make sure that everyone knows what the school is trying to achieve and what their role should be? Is it too much to expect that each person should be given the chance of inputting their perspective on what they need to develop at the same time as receiving feedback? All stakeholders in the school must want to ensure that every penny is well spent. Without an appraisal system for all, combined with a monitoring and evaluation system for all aspects of school life, we do not have this information.

Some schools are totally committed to staff development and to becoming a learning organisation where the teacher appraisal system is being supplemented by a developmental needs review system for teachers and support staff. The argument in favour of two systems is that of preserving the confidential aspects of the teacher appraisal system. A duplication of this nature may however be an unnecessary use of time, bearing in mind that under Regulation 14 (2) those responsible for planning the training and development of teachers shall receive particulars of any targets for action relating to training and development. Hence the staff development coordinator ought to be in receipt of all targets for action within their remit, whether from teachers or support staff. We would argue that coordinators should also have full knowledge of the school development plan budget and thus be in a strong position to match needs with resources.

Appraisal for all is a possibility and in an increasing number of schools it is becoming a reality. As with so many things it needs a firm commitment and priority from those in the school responsible for ensuring that visions become realities. Part of this process must involve governing bodies. In a number of cases governors are unaware of the potential and benefits of appraisal for teachers, let alone support staff. A further aspect of the role of the governors must concern equality of opportunity. Without appraisal for all, it will remain rhetoric rather than reality.

In concluding this section we recommend the following process by which to offer appraisal to all:

- a school staff development policy that offers development opportunities to all;
- a policy which enables all staff to move towards benefiting from being an appraiser and the opportunity of receiving training for this;
- effective cost-benefit analyses of providing real appraisal time for all, with this built into the school development plan;
- a public and visible commitment from the headteacher and governors to appraisal for all;
- one member of staff having an overall management responsibility for appraisal for all, and continuous professional development arrangements;
- a climate being created in the school in which appraisal is seen as a useful process which helps learning for all. This will only be achieved if people see results, which will only occur if processes are managed, people are motivated and resources, however slender, are used to meet organisational and individually identified needs;
- proper monitoring and evaluation takes place of development activities and their benefit to the individual and the organisation;
- feedback is provided which leads to future learning so that schools and individuals do not fall into the trap of learning nothing while forgetting nothing.

The questions raised for appraisal for all and the IIP initiative are clearly relevant to newly qualified teachers.

HEADTEACHER APPRAISAL

There are certain differences between headteacher and teacher appraisal which need to be addressed.

Two appraisers

The use that headteachers have made of their two appraisers has varied enormously. Some LEAs were originally very prescriptive as to the roles of the two appraisers, with the headteacher appraiser having a far greater role in the process than the officer/adviser. Other LEAs quite simply stated that as long as both appraisers were present for the initial meeting and interview, as required by law, it was up to the trio to decide on their individual roles.

There has been great variation in what has happened in practice, with some appraisers playing a large part in the process and others having a very limited role. One of the major reasons for this has been the advent of OFSTED inspections. Just as the LEA representatives were becoming closely involved with the headteacher process, many found themselves involved in inspection training and then inspections. As this was added to their existing work it left little time for headteacher appraisal. Many have, to their credit, persevered with their appraiser role and played a significant part in the process, adding a different dimension from that of the headteacher appraiser. Where this has not happened it has led to disappointments and frustrations. Similarly, some carefully planned meetings and observations have met the same fate, as a result of headteacher appraisers needing to attend to higher priorities.

As the process moves into its second cycle such issues need to be addressed, especially in those LEAs where the number of officers and advisers suitable to be headteacher appraisers has declined. We would add the following thoughts to the debate.

There needs to be a full discussion between the three participants as to how the process has worked so far, what its successes and failures have been and how each person feels about it. This discussion needs to address the issue of whether the three wish to continue working together in a second cycle or whether changes are needed. The whole issue of who the non-headteacher appraiser is also needs to be examined, especially if LEA representatives are not going to be as available the second time around. Various suggestions have been made by headteachers as to who this person should be. These have ranged from a member of the governing body, through an expert in the chosen focus area, to a colleague on the staff. Whoever the person is they should have credibility in the eyes of the appraiser and appraisee and have an appropriate level of knowledge and skill to contribute to chosen focus areas. There is likely to be considerable debate in the near future as to the role of the non-headteacher appraiser. Any change to involve someone different from an LEA officer/adviser will, at least in the case of an LEA school, need LEA sanction. GM schools, where the governing body is already responsible for such matters, will continue to make their own decisions as they have been doing in the current round of appraisals.

If a second appraiser is going to be someone related to the focus there is the presupposition that the appraisee has decided on a focus at a very early stage. This may not always be possible.

Once the match has been made there needs to be a clear understanding of the role each person will play. This has sometimes not been the case in the past and has led to confusion. Each role needs to be clearly defined in terms of time needed and tasks involved. Ground rules need to be laid, for example to identify situations which can cause the postponement of an agreed meeting and the mechanisms for people keeping in touch with each other. An initial meeting with a tight agenda, held away from the school, is one of the most successful ways of achieving this. Perhaps even more crucial is the commitment each person has to the process and a clarity as to its purpose. Unless all three participants can see where the appraisal fits into the day-to-day job of the headteacher the likelihood of success is diminished.

The headteacher appraisal focus

As with teachers, focus areas chosen by heads have been varied and many. Some have 'played safe', others have been willing to risk more. It is fair to say that those heads with clear areas of focus, having a positive link with their specific roles in school, have gained more from the appraisal process. One thing that is important is that the focus areas need to be manageable and clearly understood by all three participants. There is no room here for confusion, nor for focus areas from which heads cannot see progress in their work. We would suggest that at least one headteacher focus should always have a direct relationship with a priority area of the school development plan. In a nutshell, the headteacher should focus on an area of work in which they want significant improvement, affirmation and progress.

In coming to agreement on a focus it is useful to ask for five Ws and one H:

- What is the focus?
- Why is this a focus?
- Who will do what in working on it?
- When will the activities be completed by?
- Where will observation and data collection take place?
- How will it contribute to the head's work in a positive way?

Clear and direct answers to these questions, combined with good ground rules and a realistic timetable, should ensure a meaningful process.

Target setting for headteachers (and teachers!)

Our work with headteachers has shown that all too often targets have been something latched on at the end of the interview, almost as a chore. This is not how it should be. When a focus is being chosen, the appraisee headteacher should consider what possible targets may emerge. Obviously this is not something that can, or should, be done in detail, but at least some thought should be given to this link between focus and possible target setting. Some thought also needs to be given to the roles which can be played by the two appraisers. We would recommend that as the appraisal process continues, these thoughts can be refined, so that the targets emerge from the process with meaning. If targets are to be really useful they must live in the day-to-day reality of the headteacher's job. Targets must be SMART (see p. 40). Targets must also encompass the five Ws and one H referred to earlier. Included in target setting should be milestones: points to celebrate when achieved. They should have rewards for achievements and inquests for non-achievements. Targets should be dynamic, they should add to a headteacher's life and they should be shared between the appraisee and the appraisers. Effective targets should provide satisfaction and challenge.

If targets are set as an ongoing process throughout appraisal there is more chance that they will be met. Perhaps one way of looking at targets for headteachers, and teachers too, is to consider them as long, medium or short term, as well as individual, departmental or management group, and whole school.

One of the main reasons that targets for headteachers seem to fall by the wayside is that too little attention is paid to who is responsible for their achievement, with the result that it is all left to the appraisee. If the five Ws and one H model is followed in detail this should not happen.

Headteacher appraisal as an example to others

In all aspects of school life the headteacher is looked to for example. Appraisal is no different. If a headteacher regards appraisal as an expensive waste of time this will be transmitted to the staff. We feel that headteachers and teachers cannot afford to view appraisal in this way, as there are too many other things to do. If the headteacher shows little enthusiasm for linking appraisal with staff development and with school development planning then it is unlikely that other teachers will be bothered.

Equally, if headteachers feel that they are not getting a fair deal from their appraisers then resentment will set in and again be transmitted to other staff.

There are ways to prevent this:

- We suggest that the school has a policy and code of practice outlining how appraisal will operate.
- A school should monitor and review the usefulness of appraisal in achieving its stated aims.

- Appraisal should help teachers in their day-to-day work and be seen to do so.
- Targets should visibly move things on.
- Headteacher appraisal should give a lead in all the above.

7

From Rhetoric to Reality (What the punters think!)

Primary school teacher

I understood the aim of appraisal was to enhance the quality of learning for children through a continuous and systematic process intended to help both appraiser and appraisee work out the 'next steps' for the benefit of both themselves and the organisation.

It was only after having been nominated as an appraiser that I undertook somewhat limited training in order to develop my knowledge.

One of the first statements I came across when attempting to understand the appraisal process was: 'the demands made of appraisers should be reasonable.' Being the first member of staff in my establishment to have such a role, I suggested to the headteacher I might require a reprioritisation of work and reduction of other activities. He laughed!

The benefits of appraisal appeared fourfold: those for the pupils; teachers; establishment; and the local education authority. As I began preparing for an initial meeting with the appraisee (within directed time!) I questioned my expectations of the appraisal cycle – would it assist teachers in realising their potential and thus improve the quality of education for pupils?

The initial meeting began somewhat tensely, both parties being wary and unsure, but as a positive open climate emerged so did our mutual trust and acknowledgement of each other's professionalism. We took the opportunity to check our understanding of the purposes and process of appraisal before establishing terms of reference and agreeing on arrangements for task observation and a timetable for the appraisal cycle.

I was fortunate that a 'good' relationship existed between myself and the appraisee. We already conveyed respect, empathy and genuineness which was just as well since I was busy concentrating on those other qualities required of an appraiser such as listening and questioning skills, negotiation and constructive feedback.

Thinking I had prepared adequately for the task observation, collected relevant data and clearly understood my role, I entered a classroom of Year 2 children. The atmosphere was relaxed and friendly. However, I initially felt restrained at not being able to offer assistance to the children. As my role changed and the observation became more participative (as previously negotiated) both parties felt acceptably comfortable.

The reviewing process went just as the textbooks predicted with a discussion of the present which in turn led to talking about past experiences, based on the data collection and self-appraisal elements of the appraisal process. It felt great to give feedback and recognition of achievement and successes, and to discuss and share future action to be taken in order to achieve professional and/or career developments and aspirations.

It's now the last week of the summer term. Everyone's getting ready for the holiday break and I'm busy drawing up a draft statement and preparing for a move to another establishment in the autumn. Certainly not the ideal time to complete an appraisal cycle, but it did get finished, targets were agreed and the final document was filed by the headteacher for safe keeping.

Who did benefit from the appraisal? (Apart from me of course!)

Primary deputy head

Working within the Regulations and Circular 12/91, and the school appraisal structure, I took the opportunity of taking two appraisers and two areas of focus. The headteacher, who of course had to be one appraiser, was to focus on my management role, particularly for managing meetings, while a teaching colleague who is the maths coordinator was my second appraiser and focused on an aspect of my teaching which was around maths.

We agreed that both appraisers would be present for the whole of the initial meeting and while there were two focuses we would keep the appraisal as much a common process as possible. At the initial meeting we agreed that there would be two observations of staff meetings that I was running, and data would be collected from members of staff present at the meeting about my management of it. There would be two classroom observations focusing on my maths teaching but no data collection for this part of the process.

In the staff meetings the headteacher would observe me on the following:

- a clear introduction to the meeting;
- my use of interpersonal skills during the meeting;
- time I gave for people to respond to the ideas I had;
- the use I made of eye contact;
- how I ensured everyone could participate;
- my pacing of the meeting and time keeping;
- how I concluded the meeting.

The two staff meetings which were identified were those where I was leading discussions on developing a behaviour policy for the school. As part of the observation, the headteacher took notes during the meeting to feed back to me later. Other staff were not aware that these notes were part of my appraisal until after the observations had been completed. The maths coordinator knew, of course.

Following the meetings four colleagues – a welfare assistant, two teachers new to the school and a teacher who had been at the school prior to both myself and the head – were identified and asked to offer data. They all agreed. The data was provided through individual interviews conducted by the headteacher using the same questions for each person.

The classroom observations took place in normal teaching time when I was working on maths and focused on:

- the transition of one activity to another, eg the start and explanation of the activity and the actual 'doing' of the activity;
- the time management aspect of my planning. I was operating five maths groups, so questions such as 'Do I spend appropriate amounts of time with each group?' were asked.

Each of the two classroom observations lasted 40–45 minutes, and the maths coordinator made notes as part of the observation. The classroom observations took place in the same month as the staff meetings were being observed. Following all four observations, each appraiser spent about 15 minutes asking me for my initial thoughts and giving me immediate, informal feedback. The notes made during the observations formed the basis of this dialogue. Information gathered through data collection was not fed back until the appraisal interview.

A week after the final observation, all three of us to met off site for the appraisal interview. The headteacher had drawn up a draft agenda for the meeting which was agreed by all and this included the maths coordinator making notes during the discussion between the head and myself, and the head making notes during the discussion between the maths coordinator and myself. This is not to say the discussions were only two way – all three joined in at all times. These notes formed the basis of the appraisal statement and from them the targets also emerged.

A couple of targets which emerged connected with my management role were:

- pre-reading materials to be provided for all staff, including aims and objectives of the meetings, so that staff can be better prepared, and therefore save time;
- allow more time at the end of meetings for pulling together and summarisation of themes to ensure that all staff feel their contribution has been included.

Overall, I certainly felt that in terms of my management focus and my classroom teaching the appraisal process helped me move forward. I am certain that my teaching and the learning of the children was both indirectly and directly improved as a result of my appraisal.

Primary headteacher

Focus: the school development plan – consultation and communication
One of the most difficult aspects of my appraisal was choosing what to be appraised on. This wasn't because I am good at most things – or because I am hopeless at everything. It was more trying to find the most useful area to develop in a job description that formally involves every Education Act from 1944 onwards and informally involves such things as checking a cistern lid that fell on the postman's head! At the time of diminishing LEA influence the LEA have been excellent in the approach and support to appraisal. In the *Headteacher Handbook*, issued by the LEA, a wonderful 'prompt list for the selection of possible areas of appraisal focus' was invaluable. Under the role heading, 'Policy maker and professional leader', comes School Development Plan (Staff and Related) and further along Home/ school communication, pupil involvement in decision making. The role heading of communicator 'Human relations' also provided other linked ideas – areas that perennially worry – am I really consulting, communicating, leading...? The school plan seemed to encompass much of this but was too wide a focus. How the school plan came about, who was involved and consulted, who its audience was and how it was communicated, seemed more manageable. It could also provide some insight into consultation and communication generally throughout school.

As a focus this would allow for some research by the appraisers as part of their information gathering. I see the school plan as a central tool for action during the year with some indicators for the future. It has also become a measure by which governors view my work as headteacher. Governor subcommittees are organised under School Plan headings and my termly report comments on each section.

Appraisal is a developmental process – development for the individual and for the school. It is not supposed to be threatening or worrying. It is carried out by supportive professionals and peers who understand the pressures of the job, day to day. Fine, no problem. Especially when the initial meeting was in the Forte Hotel over coffee and cakes. But then when the list of people – the 'body' of evidence – was drawn up, I began to sweat a little. The chairman of governors, an outspoken and eccentric parent governor, a new teacher, children... Well you're never quite sure what they're going to say. I knew what I thought they should say. I seem to remember going through the process of consultation in the way I said I had. But... would they remember that? It was uncomfortable. A list of questions went out. My appraisers arrived in school and were fed chocolate biscuits. Time and space were set aside for them to talk to my teacher, children and the eccentric governor (she doubled as a parent). I think they met my chairman in a local pub one evening. I didn't dare ask.

If the most difficult part was the choosing of a focus then the most challenging part was the human element of the evidence collection. The start of our professional discussion was more like the debriefing after a job interview – at the point when you're not sure if the job's yours and they're telling you politely to try again – or somewhere else. It soon settled to a professional yet informal discussion. All the positive points came out first: 'perceived to be a good listener, consulted with people and acted on comments, appropriate and beneficial consultation, plan regularly referred to...' Then the points for improvement 'process a little too rushed, start earlier, clarify its audience, prioritise statements, revise methods of costing, how flexible is it?, clarify evaluation...'

I signed the 'Record of discussion' notes. I made my comments on the 'thoroughness and fairness of the process' and was asked to write my own targets, pass them on to my appraisers (by whom they were duly signed) and get ready for my action, with a review date arranged six months hence. The appraisal so far had taken me through four meetings (at two hours each, maximum), phone calls to set up the meetings and an hour or so to write up the targets. The appraisers spent considerably more time interviewing, note taking, transcribing and liaising.

It wasn't a comfortable, easy process. It wasn't a soft-touch approach (as most of my governors think compared to their hard-nosed business appraisals). It was handled very professionally. It has been an extremely useful way of reflecting on process and practice.

It forced me to take time to do this. I don't know how I'm going to find the time or the nervous energy to do it again. But I will, because we do, and not always because we have to.

Secondary main scale teacher

Preparation for appraisal began on my first ever professional development day, which was devoted to overcoming assumed resistance to the new procedure. The headteacher took the valiant line of 'I'll go first chaps!' while others clearly thought women and children should have the privilege. As a very newly qualified teacher still wondering how to cope *without* observations, the level of anxiety seemed surprising. Later preparation took the form of three group sessions explaining the appraisal cycle and both generating and calming pre-appraisal tension.

My own appraisal became due in my third year, shortly after a school inspection. This timing seemed excellent: I was not too old to be observed but was finally wise enough to ask my own questions, none of which had been answered by inspection. There seemed to me no shortage of 'problem areas' inviting a spot of professional self-flagellation but, mindful of advice to ask questions with possible answers, I resisted the temptation of 'What am I doing wrong with Year 11 on rainy Friday afternoons?' Better, I felt, to look at an aspect of work that I enjoyed but where I had no previous feedback: my sixth form teaching had never been observed nor much discussed and students at that stage no longer give instant unambiguous, feedback.

In the pre-observations meeting with my appraiser I explained my questions and what I thought she ought to see happening in the lessons. Having done this, it was relatively easy to make it happen. Otherwise my planning was only affected in that I prepared the two lessons as a distinct block. The students were told that we were comparing techniques in the English and French departments and were happy to be promised that Ms X wouldn't understand a word anyway. Just say it fast and keep smiling, I assured them, she'll think you're wonderful. And she did. Her appreciative comments to the students at the end of the lesson were a treat for us all. The morale boost for the students was a bonus I had not anticipated but much appreciated. Moral: let your students show off to someone who knows less than they do!

Oral feedback to me was immediate and cheerful. The written Appraisal Statement was particularly useful in that my appraiser knew the students' work in her own department so I could rely on her assessment of their efforts and reactions (even if she hadn't understood a word!). This direct comparison was a great help and suggested one of my targets: visiting other departments to make more comparisons for myself. The other targets arose more from discussions than the observations. One which required me to take a course outside school has been achieved. Another I was chivvied into pursuing at my interim review, but the two which involve extra work with other staff who *don't* have the same targets remain, not surprisingly, wishful thinking. Perhaps this shows the danger of targets being own goals?

Whereas the formal targets have not all been achieved (yet?), the personal benefit of positive feedback for myself and my students has been invaluable. Even on those rainy Friday afternoons!

Secondary head of department (Drama)

I must admit to suffering from the usual initial fears and apprehensions about appraisal in school. This was partly because of scaremongery in the press, highlighting 'teacher sackings' as a direct result of appraisal and also because of some of the models currently in use in industry, which tend to be judgemental and often crude. It seemed to be just another time-consuming pressure to cope with and, quite frankly, a potentially threatening experience. I was pleasantly surprised, therefore, when I was introduced to the Cumbrian model for teacher appraisal which gives the appraisee control over the procedure and seemed to aim to build on the positive rather than dwell on the negative. At the time I remember feeling that this was something we had to do and the choice seemed to be either to pay lip-service to it or to do it in a more committed way and perhaps achieve something positive from it. Pilot schools certainly seemed to have found the experience a positive one.

I was trained as a trainer for our staff by Charlotte Mason College, using the Cumbrian model, and then went on to train primary school staff in the county. My own experience of appraisal turned out to be, on balance, a worthwhile experience. Instead of using the rather cumbersome negative preference system of choosing appraisers suggested in the Cumbrian model our managers decided to allocate an appraiser to each member of staff. This seemed to work for most colleagues and those who were dissatisfied were given the option to change after discussion with the appraisal coordinator. As a head of department, my appraiser was a member of the management team but I was given the opportunity of having a colleague from my own department to deal with classroom observation. I chose to do this because I felt that a fellow practitioner would know what to look for. In future, however, I think that I could benefit from an outsider's point of view as there is always the possibility of developing a house style within the department. I also feel that senior managers should have first-hand experience of the work done in the department.

My appraiser behaved in a businesslike but completely non-threatening way and guided me through the process sensitively and efficiently. One of the most worthwhile experiences, surprisingly, was the self-review, which I seriously considered not doing at all. As teachers, I suppose we are so busy trying to keep our heads above water most of the time, that we rarely give ourselves time to reflect on what we actually do. The self-review, while seeming rather self-indulgent, did allow me to focus on weaknesses but, more importantly perhaps, strengths for a change. We tend to be very self-critical in our profession, we never feel that we are doing enough for every child but this exercise at least makes you stop and look at the positive aspects of your work.

The other most helpful aspect of the procedure was target setting in a systematic and organised way. If anyone had asked me before appraisal whether I set myself targets I would have said 'Yes', but I had never really stuck to target dates or been entirely realistic about their relevance or measurability. I actually chose six targets and managed to meet them. Next time I think that three or four would be more appropriate. Knowing that there was going to be a review meeting spurred me on to trying to meet the targets; without that, it would have been easy to find excuses for not completing them.

Classroom observation should not have been a worry for me, with years of experience and also recent involvement in the school's quality assurance programme, but I must admit to feelings of apprehension. I worried needlessly. My colleague made accurate and non-judgemental notes, focusing on the agreed areas and using the agreed criteria. We discussed the evidence as two professionals immediately after the lessons and I found it a valuable learning experience. It was interesting to find that we shared similar problems we hadn't discussed before, even though we have worked together for a number of years, and because of this we were able to work out strategies for tackling them. It was also very gratifying to have strengths pointed out by a fellow practitioner. This way of working seems to me to be much more valuable than the OFSTED-style monitoring system which is being introduced into our school, post-inspection.

As a vehicle for staff development, I don't know whether appraisal helped me, though I have been given a temporary post of responsibility since. In order for staff development to occur as a direct result of the appraisal process in our school, the appraisal statements need to be given to the staff development officer (also the appraisal coordinator) rather than the head.

I am at present undergoing the second cycle of my appraisal and this time it is tending to be less stringent, perhaps because I have the same appraisers. It could also be because the government appears to have remained silent on the issue for some time and colleagues are speculating about appraisal being replaced by systematic monitoring. I think that would be a retrograde step, since appraisal is based on trust and building on the positive. Any system which raises the self-esteem of teachers must be helpful, in a profession where low morale is becoming increasingly more prevalent.

Secondary head of department (Science)

My introduction to formalised appraisal was in the summer term of 1990 when I was asked to take part in a funded pilot scheme at Haydon Bridge High School, Northumberland.

My motivation for volunteering for this venture into the unknown was mainly that I had recently been appointed to the role of head of Science and I felt that it would be very useful to have an independent assessment of how effective I had been in my first year of the job. Interestingly, my partner in crime for the exercise was an English and Drama teacher who was also equal opportunities coordinator within the school. In order to complete the project with minimal disruption to our teaching commitments but still experience all aspects of the appraisal process it was decided that I should appraise my colleague on classroom skills but she should focus on my managerial role only.

We both undertook a lot of information gathering by interviewing staff and students and I observed two English lessons. I found the exercise fascinating. It was really interesting to see the skills, processes and problems in a subject area totally different from my own. In terms of the focus of the observation (gender bias and transition from GCSE to A Level) my lack of specialist subject knowledge was not an issue at all.

So what actually emerged from the exercise? First, I would say that as colleagues we developed a lot of trust and respect for each other that has endured and been of value on many occasions since. Second, there is no doubt that independent observation can bring to the fore important issues that otherwise would remain unnoticed or unspoken. In the hurly-burly of the classroom situation even the best teacher in the world will miss things that an observer will easily pick up. Similarly, departmental colleagues will say things to a person from 'outside' that they would be unlikely to say so directly face to face. *[Please note that the two examples just mentioned could be referring to either positive or negative aspects of a teacher's performance.]*

This brings us inevitably to the fears that tend to surround the dreaded appraisal. In the early days there was a great deal of resentment and ill feeling towards appraisal and the motivation behind it. Even the staff who have approached appraisal professionally and positively have found it difficult to come to terms with the concept of having someone sitting in on lessons, often with pen and notebook in hand. In some subject areas, such as Science and Art, teachers and students have grown accustomed to familiar faces wandering in and out of lessons and after a while it becomes a natural and accepted situation. Nevertheless I feel that however often staff and students are appraised, or indeed inspected, I can never envisage a time when an observer in the classroom will not affect the behaviour and performance of the teacher and the student. (Any physicists reading this will instantly recognise an example of Heisenberg's uncertainty principle!)

Personally my answer to members of staff who are worried about observation is quite simple. Personal and political views should be swept aside in the classroom, even the less inspiring and talented teacher should be able to produce one or two really special lessons if they can switch on to the fact that the motivation for doing so might be, on the one hand increased promotion prospects, on the other a favourable inspection report for the department and the school. The fact that two or three observed lessons does not give the full picture is of course totally true but irrelevant. If that is the system then we all have to learn to make the best of it. It is to be hoped that even the most negative of teachers will at some stage derive some benefit from the process but of course that is entirely in their own hands.

I feel that the number of teachers with strong negative feelings about the concept of and motivation behind appraisal has decreased to a relatively small number as the appraisal system has got into full swing. However, I do feel that enthusiasm for appraisal is at a very low level. The 'threat' aspect has all but disappeared and many teachers are saying that it is so non-threatening as to be virtually a waste of time. There is a close parallel here with 'Records of Achievement' for students. It seems that the appraisee is in the main setting the agenda, and the appraiser is confined to positive comments in the appraisal statement. This is a serious problem and needs to be addressed if credibility is to be achieved.

It is imperative that teachers do not feel that appraisal is a waste of time, since time is something that the modern teacher has very little of. As a head of department I tended to have at least two appraisals or reviews pending at any one time as well as my own annual appraisal/review. As the process got into full swing I tried to remain as professional as possible but I have to admit that as tasks were mounting and the pressure was on, appraisal as an item that did not have immediate impact on student performance tended to get pushed to the back of my stacking system, and I was not able to meet deadlines. Many other members of staff found themselves in the same situation. Frankly in the present climate I do not know what the answer is. Teachers have little time and although separate funding is available for supply cover, I and many others like me are averse to leaving our students with baby-sitters when we ought to be teaching them. The system will only work when appraisal is integrated into the structure of the timetable and this really could only happen when staffing and funding are brought back to the levels of 20 years ago.

To summarise, I feel that appraisal is right and necessary both for the professional development of the individual and for the successful management of a school. If those two things are in order then the prospects for better education of our students is there. Surely it is every teacher's wish to perform at maximum efficiency. For appraisal to succeed the process needs tightening up to increase its credibility and worth. As is true for most things in education today, it needs proper planning and funding at source.

Secondary deputy head

As a deputy head I have been involved with appraisal from its beginning. In the course of the last five years I have seen a change in teacher attitudes towards this, from one of suspicion and hostility to one of acceptance and a general belief in it as a positive help in the improvement and widening of educational expertise.

At the outset I felt that what I was given to do was to me more of a professional review than appraisal. This was the basis of the introductory talks which I held when explaining to colleagues what was about to happen and more importantly how it was to be conducted. I felt then and am now even more convinced that the improvement of teacher effectiveness, whatever else one likes to call it, must be based on mutual trust and respect plus a genuine desire by all involved to improve teaching techniques and management skills. After four years 'professional review and development' is our adopted title for what is officially called appraisal.

The outcome of the reviews so far is very encouraging in many ways. For individual teachers it offers opportunities not only to talk and analyse their own immediate practice but enables them to gain insight into other areas of the school in which they would not normally be involved. Our system being cross-curricular is particularly helpful in achieving this. In an independent evaluation of the reviewing process to date a significant number of teachers saw the time set aside, in which to discuss with a colleague matters important to themselves, as a unique and extremely valuable experience.

The professional review and development process, and the positive attitudes it has engendered, resulting in benefits for individual and school development, is threatened by the recent cessation of GEST funding to support appraisal. The prime concern must be to find the necessary funding to enable the successful aspects of this work to continue.

School development planning is of great importance, and the professional review and development process in school is fundamental to that process. A lot of time has been spent in getting the above linked and integrated with the financial planning required. Too much time and effort has been invested and too much achieved to allow a breakdown to occur.

8

Tips for Successful Appraisal

Self-Appraisal

Should be meaningful
Should be related to your job
Should be related to your past experience
Should be related to your future ambitions
Use any self-appraisal prompt sheets or documents you feel
comfortable with
Think of your needs in the organisation
Think of your personal needs
Try to link the two
Be analytical and honest with yourself
Use self-appraisal to help you arrive at a focus
Avoid the confessional attitude!
Think about what you want out of the appraisal process
Think about what you want to be different as a result of your
appraisal
Think about what this difference will look like
Think about training and development implications
Think about the quality of your teaching
Think about the quality of the pupils' learning

Initial meeting

Agree the date, time, place and duration between the appraisee
and the appraiser
Choose a suitable venue
Choose an undisturbed environment
The venue does not have to be in school!
Be on time

Have an agenda and stick to it
Agree who will keep notes
Keep accurate records
Agree challenging and rigorous focuses
Agree all the details of observation
Agree all the details of other data collection
Agree your ground rules for conducting the appraisal

Setting a focus

Consider school, departmental, team or group priorities
Consider your individual priorities
Try to cover both
Make sure your focuses are SMART
Learn from the first cycle of appraisal
There is no rule as to how many focuses you have

Observation

Make sure the observation is directly related to the focus
Be clear as to how the observation will take place
Agree ground rules for the observation
Agree the role of the observer
Decide when the observer will enter and leave the classroom
Be clear what you are going to tell the pupils
Be clear how any recording will take place
Allow time for informal feedback after the observation
Feedback should always be constructive
Observation should contribute to the appraisal interview

Data collection

Data collection should be related to the focus
All aspects of data collection should be agreed between appraiser and appraisee
Data collection should be manageable
Data does not always have to be written
Data collected should contribute to the interview
Agree what will happen to any written data
Only agreed data should be collected

The appraisal interview

Agree on the date, time, place and duration of the interview
Stick to your agreements!

Choose a comfortable, undisturbed environment
Interviews do not always have to be on school premises
Agree who will take notes
Agree what will happen to them
Be constructive in your feedback
The appraisee should offer feedback to the appraiser on how they are performing as appraisers
Write the statement in the interview if possible – it saves time
Agree the targets in the interview with an action plan to meet them

Targets

Targets should be as SMART as the focus!
Targets should have performance indicators
Targets should be rigorous
Targets should be individually developmental
Targets should be related to departmental, team and school development plans
Targets should be monitored
Targets should be met
Targets should be evaluated
Targets should be challenging
Targets should make a difference to what happens in you day-to-day life in school
Targets should improve the quality of teaching
Targets should improve the quality of learning
Targets should improve school effectiveness
Target successes should be celebrated

Bibliography

Advisory Conciliation and Arbitration Service (ACAS) (1986) Teachers' Dispute, ACAS Independent Panel Report of the Appraisal/Training Working Group, ACAS CAI.

Barber, Michael, Evans, Alan and Johnson, Michael (1995) 'An Evaluation of the National Scheme of School Teacher Appraisal', Department for Education and Employment, London.

Department of Education and Science (DES) (1991) Circular 12/91, 'School Teacher Appraisal', DES, London.

Department for Education (DfE) (1992) Circular 2/92, 'Induction of Newly Qualified Teachers', DfE, London.

Department for Education and Employment/Office for Standards in Education (DfEE/OFSTED) (1995) 'Framework for the Inspection of Schools', HMSO, London.

'Education (School Teacher Appraisal) Regulations 1991', No. 1511, HMSO, London.

Fullan, M G (1992) *Successful School Improvement*, Open University Press, Buckingham.

Harris, Dr A and Russ, J (1995) *Pathways to school improvement*, Department of Employment, London.

Morris, Bob (ed) (1991) *Local Education Authorities Project* (LEAP) 'Appraisal in Schools', BBC, London.

National Steering Group (1989) *School Teacher Appraisal – A National Framework*, HMSO, London.

Newton, Malcolm and Mack, Valerie (1994) 'The INSET Impact' *Managing Schools Today*, Vol. 3, No. 5, pp 30–32.

Oliver, Paul (1992) 'Quality in the Classroom: Philosophical aspects of measuring teacher effectiveness', *The Vocational Aspects of Education*, Vol. 44, No. 2, pp 183–90.

Pierce, Anthony (1995) 'Appraisal: Roles and results', *Managing Schools Today*, Vol. 4, No. 7, pp 34–5.

Pierce, Anthony (1994) 'Hitting Performance Targets', *Managing Schools Today*, Vol. 4, No. 9, pp 20–21.

Stoll, L and Fink, D (1992) 'Effecting school change: The Halton approach', *School Effectiveness and School Improvement*, Vol. 3, No. 1 pp 19–41.

Stoll, L and Mortimore, P (1995) *Viewpoint No. 2*, Institute of Education, London.

van Velzen, W, Miles, M, Ekholm, M, Homeyer, V and Robin, D (1985) *Making School Improvement Work: A Conceptual Guide to Practice* , Acco Publishers, Leuven, Belgium.

Washington, Kenneth (1993) 'Teacher Initiated Staff Development: What do principals and teachers think?' *School Organisation*, Vol. 13, No. 3, pp 251–3.

Index

www.ingramcontent.com/pod-product-compliance
Ingram Content Group UK Ltd.
Pitfield, Milton Keynes, MK11 3LW, UK
UKHW020855280225
455677UK00006B/50